ESSAY WRITING

A Guide To Essay Structure
&
Different Rhetorical Patterns

D1371730

by

Kenneth P. Cash

Easy-to-understand book layout and explanations

Seekers Publishing, Inc.
P.O. Box 31630
Independence, Ohio 44131

ISBN: 978-0-615-18046-5

Library of Congress Control Number: 2007909742

Front cover artwork: Angelie Mar Marrero Agosto

Book printed by: DeHART's Media Services, Inc., Santa Clara, CA 95054

Dedication

This book is dedicated to
Missy
Ms. Melissia S. Lowery

About the Author

Kenneth P. Cash

Instructional Specialist for English
at Cuyahoga Community College

Instructor of English
at Cuyahoga Community College

Co-host of Grammar Television Show
at Cuyahoga Community College

President of Seekers Publishing, Inc.

Kenneth P. Cash has been tutoring several English, Speech, and English as a Second Language (ESL) courses at Cuyahoga Community College (CCC), the Metropolitan Campus in Cleveland, Ohio, since 1978.

Also, for many years he simultaneously taught some of the CCC-Metro developmental and college-level English courses at CCC-Metro and elsewhere as a part-time college English instructor. He quit teaching classes to pursue his own writing.

In addition, since 2005 he has been co-hosting a television show called *The Grammar Zone*.

He holds a Bachelor of Arts degree from Cleveland State University, 1977.

He is the founder and president of Seekers Publishing, Inc.

Kenneth P. Cash

Table of Contents

Part I: Preliminaries

Introduction   p. i

Audience and Purpose   p. 2

General Guidelines For Formal Writing   p. 4

Process To Use When Writing An Essay   p. 5

General Rules For Structuring An Essay   p. 6

Various Introductory Techniques –
Getting Started When Writing Essays   p. 9

Writing Thesis Statements   p. 13

Transitional Words   p. 16

Titles   p. 18

Part II: Types of Essays

Short Approaches To Some Rhetorical Patterns   p. 20

Description   p. 21

Definition   p. 27

Exemplification (Example)   p. 33

Process p. 39

Comparison/Contrast p. 45

Classification p. 57

Cause and Effect p. 63

Argumentation p. 71

Narration p. 83

Similarities And Differences Between Essays
And Research Papers p. 92

Introduction

Sometimes college students are required to write essays using **expository prose**. **Expository** means to **explain** information. **Prose** is the style of writing using the **conventional rules of grammar and mechanics** such as avoiding sentence fragments, run-on sentences, subject-verb agreement problems, using correct punctuation, and so forth. **Prose** is the opposite of poetry which is a more artistic form of writing.

Rhetorical patterns mean different ways to **organize** information.

Using expository prose, this book will provide information about how to write an essay, parts of an essay, outlining, and explanations of various rhetorical patterns with outlines and essays. The essay structure presented in this book is what I call "traditional" essay structure. After you have become skilled in writing in different patterns within the traditional mode, you can *deliberately* break rules to achieve certain effects, but before you know how to break a grammar rule to achieve an artistic effect, first you need to learn what the rule is.

There are many correct ways to write outlines. Also, there may be more rhetorical patterns than appear in this book. It is nearly impossible, if not impossible, to write an essay that is pure, 100% one rhetorical pattern, for example an essay that is completely a cause and effect or classification. Most essays are combinations of two or more patterns, but ONE rhetorical pattern will dominate the essay or be the strongest pattern of the essay. For instance, example and description are two rhetorical patterns. However, a writer may use examples and descriptions in a comparison and contrast essay or to argue a point in an argumentative essay. Although rhetorical patterns are useful and cover many situations when writing, the rhetorical patterns presented and possible rhetorical patterns not presented in this book are not the only ways to present written information to readers. For example, a written composition may be composed to merely inform readers of something. There are many ways to write information.

Generally, when you are writing an essay from an outline, every time you start a new roman numeral (e.g. I, II, III, IV ...) on the outline, start a new paragraph in the essay.

Some of the sample essays in this book are longer than the essays you may be asked to write.

SPECIAL NOTE:

Various professionals have different theories about some of the methods of writing activities. This book contains <u>general guidelines</u> for using various rhetorical patterns. Whenever an instructor gives you an assignment, <u>follow your instructor's directions</u>.

Part I:

Preliminaries

Whenever you write anything, you need to consider two things:

Audience

and

Purpose

For whom are you writing this composition? Are you writing this composition for a certain individual or a certain group of people whom you want or expect to read what you have written?

For example: If I were a surgeon writing about a new surgical technique for removing a person's appendix, I would write that article much differently if I were writing that article for a medical journal where the readers would be other surgeons and various other medical people as opposed to writing about that same technique for *Time* magazine where the majority of readers of that article would be average people with no special knowledge of the medical field.

Also, **why** am I writing this composition?

Some examples of some reasons for writing something:
- to <u>inform</u> the reader about someone or something
- to <u>provide comfort</u> for someone
- to <u>inspire</u> people or to <u>motivate</u> people to do something, to <u>take</u> **constructive** <u>action</u> on an issue
- to <u>explain</u> how to do something
- to <u>anger</u> an audience to try to get them to take a stand or take **constructive** action on an issue
- to <u>compare and/or contrast</u> two people or two things – how are two people or two things the same and/or different?
- to <u>"set the record straight"</u> about a person, situation, or issue
- to <u>tell</u> a story
- to <u>persuade</u> a person to agree with you on an issue
- etc.

Many essays are written for the **general audience**, meaning **anybody** could read your essay.

Assume nothing!   Pretend that your reader(s) know(s) nothing about the topic that you are writing about, so you have to explain everything.

Along with that idea of explaining everyone and everything, try to remember that you may know about whom or what you are writing, but that does not necessarily mean that the reader knows about whom or what you are writing.

For example: Let's say you write the following sentence in your essay: "Sarah did the grocery shopping for my mother."

YOU may know who **Sarah** is, but the reader most likely does not know. Thus, a better way to write is the first time you mention the person, Sarah, let the reader know who Sarah is; in other words, *introduce* Sarah to the reader.

For example: "My sister, Sarah, did the grocery shopping for my mother."

Now the reader knows who Sarah is – my sister.

Then if you mention Sarah again later on in your essay, all you have to write is "Sarah," and the reader will know who Sarah is.

NOTE: If your instructor asks you to write for a certain audience, then follow your instructor's directions.

General Guidelines For Formal Writing
Be Consistent.

1. Do not use the word "you". In its place, some other possibilities include " an individual, a person, one, he, she, it."

2. Avoid the word "thing" where possible. Use a word that is more specific to your topic.

3. Do not use contractions – words like "don't, we'll, it's" unless in a quotation.

   Spell out words completely.

4. Usually write from the perspective of **third person**.

I	we
you	you
he, she, it	**they**

5. Do not begin a sentence with a coordinating conjunction (for, and, yet, so, nor, or, but).

6. Avoid "etc." Do not leave information incomplete.

7. Do not use capital letters at random. You may have to modify your penmanship.

8. Do not use slang or **informal words** like **"kids"** for "children" unless part of a quotation.

9. Do not abbreviate words (certain words excluded).

10. Do not use symbols such as "&" for "and".

11. Try not to use the words "in other words". Write it the way you want your idea to be the first time.

Process To Use When Writing An Essay

1. Choose a SUBJECT – example – Medical Profession.

2. Narrow the subject to a TOPIC – Nurses.

3. BRAINSTORM ------ List all of the ideas that come to your mind about your topic, listing them in the order that you think of them, using just one word or short phrase for each idea.

4. OUTLINE ------------- <u>Organize</u> the ideas you wrote when you brainstormed so that they relate to each other in a logical, coherent manner.

5. Write the
   ROUGH DRAFT ---- Start at the beginning of your outline and turn all words and phrases into complete sentences, in paragraph form, in the same order that the ideas appear on your outline.

6. Write the
   FINAL COPY ------- Correct all errors in rough draft like spelling, punctuation, sentence order, word choice, etc.

7. PROOFREAD
   final copy   ------- Read final copy one last time to check for errors.

Do not underestimate the importance of step #7, proofreading your written work.

Suggestion – Read last sentence first, then the second last sentence, etc., to the first sentence, not concentrating on ideas but on grammar and mechanics of writing.

General Rules For Structuring An Essay

(A <u>Traditional</u> Style)

TITLE   Includes the TOPIC of essay in it

        (Do not underline or put quotation marks around title.)

        (Capitalize the first and last words and any important word in the middle of title.)

Paragraph #1 INTRODUCTION including THESIS STATEMENT

        --- The first sentence should get the reader's attention.

        --- 2 or 3 sentences "introducing" the topic you wish to discuss in your essay – (getting the reader familiar with your topic which leads up to the thesis statement)

        (State just facts about your topic; do not include any opinions in these sentences.)

        --- The <u>thesis</u> <u>statement</u> can appear <u>anywhere</u> in the introductory paragraph, (paragraph #1), but it is many times best to place it as the <u>last</u> sentence of that paragraph.

        --- A THESIS STATEMENT is the main idea of the <u>whole</u> <u>essay</u> (all of the paragraphs together).

        --- A thesis statement is a specific statement about the topic and contains an attitude (or opinion).

        --- A thesis statement should contain 3 items:
         1) the <u>topic</u>
         2) a <u>word</u> that expresses your <u>opinion</u>
           examples: <u>best</u> school, <u>worst</u> date, <u>enjoyable</u> day,
              <u>beautiful</u> room, <u>happiest</u> time
         3) a list of (usually) 3 <u>subdivisions</u> of your topic
           example: Sharing the road with <u>excellent drivers</u> is safer than coping with <u>average drivers</u> and <u>poor drivers</u>.

          --- When stating your opinion, do not use the words "I think, I believe, in my opinion," etc.).

--- A further examination of the thesis statement:

> Sharing the road with excellent drivers is safer than coping with average drivers and poor drivers.
>
>> 1) Topic: Sharing the road with other drivers
>> 2) Opinion word: safer
>> 3) List of subdivisions:
>>> excellent drivers, average drivers, poor drivers

--- An example of another possible thesis statement:

> Kindness, gentleness, and sensitivity cause Karen to be a wonderful person.
>
>> Topic: Karen's personality
>> Opinion word: wonderful
>> Subdivisions of topic:
>>> Kindness
>>> Gentleness
>>> Sensitivity

Another way of writing the above thesis statement:

> Karen has a wonderful personality because she is kind, gentle, and sensitive.
>
>> Topic: Karen's personality
>> Opinion word: wonderful
>> Subdivisions of topic:
>>> Kind
>>> Gentle
>>> Sensitive

Paragraph #2

A main idea (topic sentence) about the thesis statement

followed by supportive evidence (details, examples about the main idea of the paragraph)

Paragraph #3 and any additional middle paragraph(s)

Repeat same procedure as in paragraph #2 for additional paragraphs.

Last paragraph   The CONCLUSION <u>should</u> <u>include</u> 2 items:

    1. Provide a <u>summary</u> (which includes the main idea of each middle paragraph).

        For example, if you have 3 middle paragraphs
        (the paragraphs between the introductory paragraph
        and the concluding paragraph), then you have
        3 main ideas.

        When repeating these ideas, try to use at least some
        different words; do not just copy the sentences
        word-for-word.

    2. <u>Restate</u> the idea presented in the <u>thesis</u> <u>statement</u>; (write the same thing you wrote in the thesis statement, but use different words if possible).

        Do NOT put into conclusion

           --- details/examples

           --- new information

                If you have not already discussed an idea in your
                essay, do not write about that idea
                in your conclusion.

                An exception might be in the argumentative essay.

Getting Started

When Writing An Essay

"I have my topic, but I don't know how to start." Did you ever say this when you tried to start writing an essay? Sometimes getting started writing those first few sentences in paragraph #1 (the introduction) is the hardest part of writing an essay.

The thesis statement is one of the sentences in the introductory paragraph (paragraph #1). The thesis statement is a <u>specific</u> statement about your topic and contains your attitude (opinion). (When you write your thesis statement, do NOT use words like "I think that," "I believe that," or "In my opinion." Just state your opinion. For example, do **NOT** write for a thesis statement, **I think** that Fords are the best cars because of quality materials, excellent engineering, and superb workmanship." JUST WRITE, Fords are the best cars because of quality materials, excellent engineering, and superb workmanship.") The thesis statement is the <u>main</u> <u>idea</u> of the <u>whole</u> <u>essay</u> (all of the paragraphs together in an essay). Although the thesis statement may be anywhere in paragraph #1, many times the thesis statement is best stated as the last sentence of paragraph #1 of an essay. You may ask, "But what do I write in paragraph #1 <u>before</u> I state the thesis statement?" An introduction should get the reader interested in your topic, so start with some sentence that will hopefully cause the reader to want to read the rest of your essay. When you are ready to begin writing an essay and you cannot think of an attention-getter or hook, just *temporarily* bypass it and begin writing the essay. When writing your essay, thoughts about your topic will hopefully come to your mind which may help you to eventually think of an attention-getter. Then, just add your attention-getter as the first sentence of your essay. Just because your completed essay will have the attention-getter as the first sentence does not mean that you have to necessarily write that sentence first when you are composing your essay. If you cannot initially think of an attention-getter, do not let that keep you from continuing to write the rest of your essay. An introduction should also get the reader familiar with your topic – provide a background for your topic before you tell the reader what your thesis statement (main idea) is.

<u>Seven ways (of many) of starting an essay are explained below</u>. You may use one method or a combination of methods when writing your introduction. The thesis statement is underlined in each example of each method to help in your understanding. However, when you write your essay, do not underline your thesis statement unless your instructor asks you to do so.

9

1. Broad to Specific

Start with a broad, general statement about your topic. Then narrow your statements to get to your thesis statement.

example:
      The medical profession includes many different groups of people who all work together to assist people with medical problems. Some of these groups of professionals consist of doctors, nurses,   and laboratory technicians. Nurses' duties entail monitoring and assisting patients. <u>Most nurses are very dedicated to their profession</u>.

The writer goes from broad to specific –

1. different groups of medical professionals
2. doctors, nurses, laboratory technicians
3. nurses

2. Define your topic

Actually, the above introductory paragraph is a combination of #1, broad to specific and definitions of the topic.

example:
      "… work together to assist people with medical problems," and "… monitoring and assisting patients."

3. Contrast (difference)

Start with information that is opposite of the idea you are going to develop in your essay. Between the two opposite ideas, put in a "contrast transition."

example:
      Sarah would become irritated no matter who interrupted her when she was doing her homework. Whether her father, mother, younger brother, or female friends interfered during her study time, Sarah was annoyed and displayed her feelings of anger. <u>However, when Sarah's boyfriend called her on the telephone as she was studying, she became very happy.</u>

4. Importance

Begin your introduction by explaining why your topic is important.

For instance, some people do not like history and think it is useless and boring.

example:

      History is vital to understanding people and societies which help people to analyze how societies function in order for people to run their own lives. In addition, history helps people to understand change and contributes to moral understanding. Studying history also provides individuals with identity and is useful in creating good businesspeople, professionals, and political leaders. Moreover, knowledge of history informs people how past actions produced certain results which provide individuals with valuable insight into current situations. <u>Thus, history should be taught as a **dramatic** record of people, places, and events.</u>

5. Brief story

Start your essay by telling a brief story, incident, event that is related to your thesis statement idea.

example:

      To attempt to demonstrate her invention of enabling people to fly in the air, a woman is wearing boards strapped to her arms and a "tail" fastened to her back. Flapping her arms up and down, she runs faster and faster on a golf course. She trips and falls down onto her back. She lies on the ground waving her arms and legs, trying to stand up, but she cannot get up. She resembles a turtle lying upside down on its shell. <u>Although some inventions are successful, many inventions are humorous failures.</u>

6. Questions

Start your essay by asking a question(s) to the reader.

example:

      Have you ever been embarrassed in front of your relatives? Do you know what it feels like? <u>Being mortified in front of your relatives is terrible.</u>

7. Quotation

Start your essay with a quotation.

example:

    "The only statesmen are dead politicians," remarked President Harry S. Truman. This decisive, assertive, and simply-spoken United States leader is an example, himself, of his statement. Truman had been the last vice president under President Franklin Delano Roosevelt. Truman suddenly became president upon the stunning death of his predecessor, President Roosevelt. Franklin Roosevelt was a very popular president (1933-1945) who was elected to that highest office four times – more times than any other person. Franklin Roosevelt suddenly died shortly before World War II ended. Thus, Harry Truman was abruptly thrust into being the central allied, world leader to successfully conclude the massive, world conflict known as World War II. Although Truman enormously helped to win World War II, during his presidency, he was considered by the general public to be a mediocre individual. Franklin Roosevelt was someone difficult to follow since Roosevelt had been so popular with so many people. <u>During Truman's presidency, although he was considered a rather ordinary person, as time has passed, over the years Truman is now generally considered to have been an extraordinary leader.</u>

Writing Thesis Statements

A **thesis statement** is the <u>main</u> <u>idea</u> of the <u>whole</u> <u>essay</u>. It should be one sentence in the introductory (first) paragraph, usually the last sentence of paragraph one.

A thesis statement is one sentence and needs to contain two or three elements or supporting points.

A thesis statement should contain these elements:

    1) the topic
    2) an opinion word
    3) two or three supporting points

        In the essay, the three supporting points should be discussed in the same order as they are presented in the thesis statement.

Here are some topics and thesis statements as examples:

1) topic: What are the primary benefits of a college or university education?

    possible thesis statement: The primary benefits of a college or university education are increased knowledge, a raised level of thinking, and more marketability.

topic:	primary benefits of a college or university education
opinion word:	benefits (implying that these three things are good)
supporting points:	increased knowledge
	raised level of thinking
	more marketability

2) topic: What famous person, living or dead, do you admire and why?

    possible thesis statement: President Abraham Lincoln deserves admiration because of his courage, compassion, and intelligence.

topic:	President Abraham Lincoln
opinion word:	admiration
supporting points:	courage
	compassion
	intelligence

3) topic: What are the advantages or disadvantages of living in a small town, a city, or the country?

    possible thesis statement: The disadvantages of living in a small town are lack of privacy, limited career potential, and limited marital choices.

topic:	living in a small town
opinion word:	disadvantages
supporting points:	privacy (everyone knows everyone else's business)
	limited career potential (not many opportunities to advance in large corporations)
	limited marital choices (a person does not have a large number of people from whom to choose when looking for someone to whom to become married)

4) topic: What is your idea of an ideal job?

    possible thesis statement: Stress free, helping people, and good pay constitute an ideal job.

topic:	ideal job
opinion word:	ideal
supporting points:	stress free
	helping people
	good pay

5) topic: If you could travel anywhere in the world, where would you most like to go and why?

    possible thesis statement: United States national parks are places where I would most like to travel to because of the parks' national beauty, uncommon features and humanly unharmed nature.

topic:	United States national parks
opinion word:	like
supporting points:	natural beauty (trees, flowers, rivers, mountains, etc.)
	uncommon features (water bubbling up from ground, huge Sequoia trees, timing of Old Faithful, etc.)
	unharmed nature (land that people have never changed. The land looks very much the same as it did when uninhabited by people.)

6) topic: What is your favorite musical group of all time and why?

possible thesis statement: The Seekers is my favorite musical group of all time because the group's songs have very strong melodies, intricate rhythm patterns, and beautiful, vocal harmony.

topic:	The Seekers – musical group
opinion word:	favorite
supporting points:	very strong melodies
	intricate rhythm patterns
	beautiful, vocal harmony

Transitions

Transitional words and phrases help readers understand the relationship between writers' ideas. Transitions help a writer to <u>smoothly</u> go from one idea to the next idea.

Think of a transitional word or phrase as a bridge between two pieces of land.

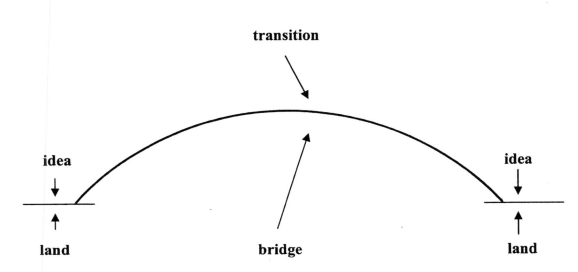

Space/
Place
here, there, beyond, yonder, near, beside, opposite, on the other side, above, beneath, to the east, eastward, to the west, westward, to the north, northward, to the south, southward, nearby, in the distance, straight ahead, at the left, at the right, in the center, on the side, along the edge on top, below, under, around, over, straight ahead, at the top, at the bottom, surrounding, opposite, at the rear, at the front, before, in front of, beside, behind, in back of, next, next to, nearby, in the distance, in the foreground, within sight, out of sight, where, wherever, in, inside, out, outside, within, through, up, down, first, second, third, (etc.), to the left, to the right, on the left, on the right

Time
immediately, soon, next, again, after a short time, at length, not long after, at last, finally, whereupon, meanwhile, then, thereafter, after a while, at the same time, simultaneously, suddenly, until, sometimes, when, whenever, while, as long as, gradually, after, before, then, at first, first, second, third, (etc.), now, last, duration, formerly, rarely, usually, another, soon, for a minute, for an hour, for a day, (etc.), during the morning, during the day, during the week, (etc.), most important, later, ordinarily, to begin with, afterward, generally, in order to

Logical Steps	next, then, to sum up, in fact, in brief, finally, in conclusion, first, second, third, (etc.)
Addition	in addition, besides, further, also, too, not only … but also, and, and then, moreover, furthermore, in like manner, likewise, similarly, in the same way, first, second, third, (etc.), next, another, as a result, consequently, finally, last, in fact, again, in other words, another point, nevertheless, nor, otherwise, then, inasmuch as, in brief, some, indeed, like, what is more
Alternate	or, nor, otherwise, if not
Comparison	some, many, all, good, better, best, much, more, most, bad, worse, worst, little, less, least, equally important
Contrast	but, though, yet, still, however, on the other hand, on the contrary, in spite of, without, here, there, then, now, nevertheless, notwithstanding, in contrast, instead, still, rather, although, even though, whereas, except, except that, after all, otherwise, conversely, while this may not be true, granted
Manner/ Condition	if, unless, lest, provided, provided that, in case, as, just as, as if, as soon as, as often as
Concession	of course, at the same time, simultaneously, I admit, for all that, after all
Purpose	for this purpose, to this end, with this in view
Cause	for, because, since, so that, due to
Result or Summary	hence, therefore, then, thus, consequently, for this reason, consequence, conclusion, accordingly, as a result, in conclusion, in summary, in general to sum up, in short, in brief, as has been (shown) (stated)
Emphasis	primarily, importantly, more importantly, most importantly, especially, more, most, less, least, surely, certainly, to be sure, undoubtedly, indeed, truly, in fact without a doubt
Example/ Illustration	for example, for instance, such as, especially, in particular, thus, to illustrate, that is, as, like, as proof, specifically, as an illustration
Repetition	in fact, in other words, differently stated
Conclusion	in conclusion, to conclude, in closing, in summary

Titles

Put **quotation marks** around the titles of **short works**.	**Underline** or **italicize** titles of long works.*
articles in books articles in magazines articles in newspapers chapters in books poems short stories songs	compact discs (CDs) titles of books titles of magazines titles of movies titles of newspapers titles of plays titles of record albums titles of television shows *In handwritten form, <u>underline</u> titles of long works. When typing on a computer, type the titles of long works in *italics*. (Do NOT do both.)

Note: Do not get confused; what determines if a title is enclosed in quotation marks, underlined or italicized is the length of the written work (the length of the PIECE OF WRITING), NOT the length of the TITLE itself. In other words, when deciding if quotation marks or underlining or italics should be used, the number of words in the title means nothing.

Part II:

Types of Essays

Short Approaches
to Some Rhetorical Patterns

X = word, words, or name being defined

Pattern of Development	Question
Definition	Can be approached in different ways What does X mean?
Description	How does X look, taste, smell, feel, and sound?
Narration	What does X do? When? Where?
Exemplification (Example)	What are some typical instances of X?
Process Analysis	How does X work?
Comparison/Contrast	What is X like or unlike?
Classification/Division	What are X's component parts? What different forms can X take?
Cause and Effect	What leads to X? What are X's consequences?
Argumentation	Why should X be agreed on?

Description

Description

When **describing** a person or thing, the writer gives the reader a **picture**, image, <u>in words</u>. Modifiers (adjectives and adverbs) are especially useful in appealing to a person's five senses – sight, hearing, taste, smell, and touch. When writing a descriptive essay, the writer should appeal to these five senses, all of which may not be appropriate depending on whom or what is being described.

Outline
(Description)

Family Reunion

I. Kindredship
    A. Talk, Visit, Socialize
    B. Hug
    C. See

II. Food
    A. Variety
    B. Amount
    C. Quality

III. Setting
    A. Field
    B. House
    C. Trees
    D. Sunny
    E. Dry

Description – Essay

Family Reunion Fun

Recalling to mind a memorable moment that occurred at a former family reunion, seventy-eight-year-old Aunt Fern tripped when quickly walking toward a picnic table, and her elderly face met with a big pie heaped with cream that was firmly sitting on a light blue picnic table. With her face covered with the fluffy mess, she heartily laughed and exclaimed, "It tastes good! Emily must have made this pie." Occasionally some nuclear and extended family members gather for what are called family reunions. These assemblages of relatives mutually socialize. Also, an abundance of scrumptious food is many times present. These gatherings can be held almost anywhere that will accommodate the number of people whom meet. Family reunions can be exceedingly fun due to kindredship, food, and a complementary setting.

Most likely the main reason to have family reunions is for relatives to enjoy blissful camaraderie. Elderly individuals, middle-aged family members, and children of all ages meet to enjoy each other's company for a period of time. Old news is caught up on along with relatives' current endeavors. At one reunion, it was learned by many attendees that Uncle Dave had had bypass heart surgery and was recovering fine although he looked a little thinner, his bones showing more than in the past. Jolly Grandma Moses had had her pesky gallbladder removed, and twenty-two-year-old Jasmine had had a precious baby boy, Jason, four months previous to the reunion. Many of the older relatives snugly hugged Jason upon meeting him. While enthusiastic adults converse, younger children playfully romp the festive grounds. At one reunion, eight high spirited children ranging from three to ten years of age cheerfully played a game of "tag," seemingly tirelessly running after each other for recreation and delightfully calling each others' names during the frolic.

Usually at family reunions, accompanying enjoyable visiting among relatives is a wide variety of enormous amounts of very tasty food! At one reunion, a bountiful smorgasbord of edibles solidly covered five, broad picnic tables. Three of the hefty benches displayed a generous multiplicity of splendid comestibles. Melissia brought a twenty inch by thirty inch, silver container of baked macaroni and cheese that contained five different kinds of delicious cheeses. There was also a humongous pot of marginally spicy baked beans. Thick, grilled hot dogs were heaped on a plate in abundance adjacent to fourteen, clear plastic bags of wiener buns made of white bread. One table held nine munificent buckets of luscious, meaty, baked and fried chicken legs, breasts, and wings covered with golden brown, zesty breading. Their appetizing aroma heavily permeated the warm air. Mounds of creamy potato salad were just waiting to be enthusiastically devoured. Party trays were present evincing a diverse assortment of cold meats including turkey, ham, beef, and baloney accompanied by an array of savory cheeses, among them mouthwatering Swiss, flavorful American, delectable provalone, and tangy cheddar, all pleasingly spread in a circle on enormous trays. Several long loaves of fresh bread sat on a broad table. There were white, dark seeded and seedless rye, brown pumpernickel and light-colored vienna bread slices that sweetly permeated the surrounding air. Next to these viands was a medley of condiments consisting of zestful salt, biting pepper, green pickle relish intermixed with small bits of pimento, titillating mustard, and agreeable, bright red ketchup, ambrosial mayonnaise, and sweet and pungent onions. Another picnic table exhibited an

24

assortment of palatable beverages. There was an enormous kettle of freshly made, cool lemonade made from real, squeezed lemons heavily sweetened with sugar and numerous chunks of ice readily floating about as the sunlight reflected off of the shiny surfaces. On the brawny table for adults also stood four tall bottles of Debonne' Vineyards chilled Razzberry Riesling, sweet, red wine with uncorked bottle tops. Adjacently lay firm paper plates, large and small drinking cups stacked, and sturdy white eating utensils. Next to the drinks was a huge chest filled with cans of various soft drinks ranging from Coca Cola to water in bottles along with cans of refreshing beer floating vicariously among the ice water. The fifth table revealed a generous assortment of tasty-looking desserts. There were exceedingly sweet pecan pies, freshly baked cherry and juicy peach pies with soft crusts, peanut butter and pumpkin pies, and delectable chocolate cakes with luscious cream frosting. A capacious aggregate of mouthwatering cookies were evinced; they included chocolate chunk cookies, exemplary frosted oatmeal cookies, and flavorful peanut butter cookies.

Furthermore, the spacious setting encompassed gently rolling hills of short, freshly-mowed, green grass with a handsome wheat field of abundant waves of three-feet high stalks plentifully cropped that smoothly swayed as the balmy, warm wind occasionally passed over the area. On the property stood an old, well-kept farm house that stood stately among the lovely chestnut, mighty oak, and elegant walnut trees where colorful birds rapturously chirped as they flitted from tree to tree. The roomy grounds were filled with delightful human sounds of lively conversation and laughter. The brilliant sun stood overhead with its radiant sunbeams brightly illuminating the lush land and arid air during the gleeful day.

Another family reunion was immensely enjoyed by all! The analogous fellowship greatly appealed to everyone present. The camaraderie was accompanied by a wide variety of delicious food in immense supply, and the day proved to be blessed with dry, splendrous sunshine throughout the grandeurous area. Family reunions can be exceptionally joyous occasions due to blissful, kind socializing, exemplary food, and splendid locations.

Definition

Definition

The definition essay is a multiparagraph writing that tells the definition (or meaning) of a word, a thing, or a person. The first place to start might be looking up the word in a dictionary. If the word has more than one meaning, choose only **one** of those meanings to expand in your essay. Do <u>not</u> write into your essay, the words, "According to Webster's dictionary _____ means _____," or anything like that.

A definition essay may begin with a simple, possibly brief, dictionary definition in your own words. Then the term being defined should be subdivided into three parts. For example, after you have a word(s) to define or explain the meaning of, like "amateur astronomer," then subdivide that term into three parts. The definition of amateur astronomer would answer this question: What do amateur astronomers say and do that cause you to know that they are amateur astronomers?

If you were to write a definition essay and your topic was Amish people, you might ask yourself, "What do Amish people say and do that cause me to know that they are Amish people? The three subcategories might be: (1) the way they dress, (2) do not use modern technology, and (3) their religious beliefs. Then you would write one paragraph about each of the three characteristics listed above. The first paragraph would briefly define the name, "Amish," with a thesis statement stating "Amish people" and the three items listed above. An outline of the three middle paragraphs might look something like this:

Topic: Amish People

I. Dress
    A. mostly black and white
    B. men – farm overalls
    C. women – long dresses
    D. plain clothes – no patterns or designs on them
    E. hats
        1. men – straw with brim
        2. women -- white bonnets

II. Non-use of and/or cannot own modern technology
    A. motorized vehicles
    B. electricity
    C. telephones
    D. washer
    E. dryer

III. Religious beliefs
    A. people select clergy
    B. every Sunday – groups at houses
    C. beards on Amish men
        1. married – does not shave – has beard
        2. unmarried – clean shaven face

Outline
(Definition)

Christian Beliefs

I. God the Father
   A. Supreme Being
   B. Creator
   C. Ruler
   D. Omniscient
   E. Omnipotent
   F. Omnipresent

II. God the Son, Jesus Christ
   A. Physical person
   B. Taught God's guidelines for living
   C. Crucified
   D. Arose
   E. Paid people's sinful debts
   F. Ascended into heaven
   G. Return on Judgment Day

III. God the Holy Spirit
   A. Provider of comfort
   B. Provider of strength
   C. Provider of inspiration
   D. Provider of spiritual energy
   E. Provider of Godly motivation
   F. Provider of Godly guidance

Definition – Essay

Special Note: Within the Christian religion, there are many denominations. Therefore, among Christians, there might be some variations of beliefs that are expressed in this essay.

Christian Beliefs

Jesus of Nazareth lived in this world for thirty-three years around two thousand years ago. According to the Holy Bible which Christians believe are writings inspired by God, Jesus Christ taught God's guidelines for living, healed the sick, and even brought back to life a man who had been dead for four days. Many Christians, all of whom are followers of Jesus Christ, are people who believe in God in three forms – God the Father, God the Son who is Jesus Christ, and God the Holy Spirit.

Christians are people who believe that God the Father exists and is the Creator of everyone and everything everywhere. Christians believe that God is a Supernatural, Supreme Being who created the universe, is omniscient (all-knowing), omnipotent (all-powerful), and omnipresent (present everywhere at the same time). Christians, people who believe in Christianity, believe that God loves people and is gracious, among the many wonderful characteristics of God. Christians also believe that God is involved in everyday dramas of people's lives. Most Christians pray (communicate with God) to God the Father in Jesus Christ's name, for Jesus Christ said, "I am the only way to God the Father."

Next, Christians are people who believe that Jesus of Nazareth is the Christ, the Messiah, the Son of the Living God and Savior of people as had been predicted by writings of the Old Testament to come into this world. The Holy Bible is the central book of Christianity. It is a collection of God-inspired writings divided into the Old Testament and the New Testament. Old Testament writings were written before Jesus Christ lived on earth, and the New Testament writings were written after Jesus Christ ascended into God's Kingdom of Heaven. While in this world, Jesus Christ taught people God's rules or guidelines for living lives that are pleasing to God. For Christians, God's rules for living Godly lives are stated in ten commandments. When asked, Jesus said that the greatest commandment is to love God completely and that the second commandment which is for people to love other people the way they love themselves is similar. Soon after God created man and woman, they sinned against God. Humankind "fell out of favor" with God because of their sinning against God. God loves people so much that He had His son, Jesus Christ, take on everyone's sins by having Jesus Christ physically die on a cross as an atonement for all of humankind's sins. Jesus Christ was crucified and physically died. On the third day afterwards, God raised Jesus Christ, and Jesus Christ was physically alive again. By Jesus Christ's crucifixion and resurrection, he paid all people's sin debts in full which made people acceptable to God and therefore opened God's kingdom of heaven, making heaven accessible to people who believe in God and believe that Jesus Christ is God's son and people's savior. Consequently, Christians believe that for a person to enter heaven, that person has to believe in God and that Jesus of Nazareth, Jesus Christ, is God's son and people's savior and that people's good works in this world will not get people into heaven but that good works can cause people to earn treasures that people can enjoy when they are living in God's Kingdom of Heaven. Christians believe that one day, called Judgment Day, Jesus Christ will return to Earth, and people will meet him in the sky where Jesus Christ will inform each person whether he or she is going to God's Kingdom of Heaven for a happy eternity or go to Hell to suffer.

The third form of God in which Christians believe is God's Holy Spirit. Before Jesus Christ ascended into heaven, he said that he would send "the Comforter," meaning the Holy Spirit. Christians believe that God's Holy Spirit lives within Christians by faith in Jesus Christ, providing Christians with comfort and strength, inspiring, energizing, and motivating Christians in the beliefs of Jesus Christ. The presence of God's Holy Spirit helps to make Christian believers loving and humble like Jesus Christ. God's Holy Spirit also guides Christians into spiritual truth and aids in leadership. When Christians believe that God's Holy Spirit is guiding them in any particular situation, Christians should examine if what they think God is directing them to do is in accordance with the Holy Scriptures because throughout the ages, many terrible acts have been committed by people who claim that God told them to do these dreadful deeds.

Christianity was born around two thousand years ago when Jesus Christ physically lived in this world for approximately thirty-three years. Christians believe that this Jesus of Nazareth is the Christ, God in heaven's son who instructed people on how to live their lives in a way that is pleasing to God the Father, the Supreme Being who created everything and is the Ultimate Ruler of everything everywhere. After Jesus Christ was crucified and was raised up by God on the third day, Jesus Christ ascended into heaven. Christ then sent God's Holy Spirit to comfort and guide Christian believers. Thus, Christians believe in God in three forms – God the Father, God the Son, and God the Holy Spirit.

Exemplification
or
Example

Exemplification (Example)

Exemplification is a derivative (another form) of the word **"example"**. In an exemplification or example essay, the writer uses examples (brief stories) to support and illustrate the idea in the thesis statement. Generally, every time the writer begins writing about a new example, the writer should start a new paragraph in the essay.

Outline
(Exemplification/Example)

Inventions

I. Garrett Morgan
    A. Gas inhalator
    B. Automatic traffic light

II. Dr. Percy Julian
    A. Physostigmine
    B. Cortisone

III. Madam C. J. Walker
    A. Madam C. J. Walker's Hair Grower
    B. Hair softeners
    C. Hair conditioners
    D. Cosmetics

Exemplification (Example) – Essay

Inventions

Inventions have been in existence nearly since humankind has occupied this world. People seek to find ways to make life easier and to progress life. In the United States, there are in excess of 152,000 patent applications that have been filed. Although many inventors of various races are not well known, African American inventors have made significant inventions that have helped to advance society.

One such inventor was Garrett Morgan who created the gas inhalator which became the gas mask and then invented the automatic traffic light. Morgan lived from 1875 to 1963. His gas inhalator became widely known on July 25, 1916 when an explosion occurred in Tunnel Number Five, which was 5 miles out and 282 feet under Lake Erie and the Cleveland Waterworks. More than 24 men were trapped in the rubble. Other men could not rescue the desperate workers because there were natural gas pockets between the men and the entrance of the tunnel. Someone remembered that Morgan had recently been demonstrating his gas inhalator to a business. Morgan was contacted, and he and his brother, Frank, assisted by volunteers, used gas inhalators as they reached the trapped men who were unconscious, and dragged the men out of the tunnel. The rescue made Morgan's gas inhalator more well known. Two years later when the United States entered World War I, poisonous gas was being used as a weapon. The United States military transformed Morgan's gas inhalator into the gas mask, saving thousands of lives in combat. Morgan is also responsible for inventing the automatic traffic light which is widely used on roads today. Morgan sold his invention to the General Electric company for $40,000. Garrett Morgan was awarded a gold medal from Cleveland, Ohio, for his devotion to public safety.

Another African American inventor, Dr. Percy Julian, who lived from 1898 to 1975, helped to create derivative drugs available to people today that ease suffering at reasonable costs. During Julian's life, he secured 86 patents, some as the sole inventor and some shared with colleagues. In 1920, Julian graduated Phi Beta Kappa from De Pauw University in Greencastle, Indiana, and was the valedictorian of his class. After teaching for several years at Fisk and Howard Universities, and Virginia State College, he attended Harvard and the University of Vienna where he received his doctorate. Then while teaching at De Pauw University, he started research. Julian's first discovery came in 1935 when he synthesized the drug physostigmine used in the treatment of glaucoma, a disease of the eye which can lead to blindness. When people at Glidden Company learned of Julian's discovery, they hired him. At Glidden Company, Julian became the director of research and the manager of fine chemicals. Then in the 1930s, Julian began researching soybeans. At this time, Europe had a monopoly on the production of sterols which are any of a group of predominantly unsaturated solid. The European monopoly created the situation of sterols costing several hundred dollars a gram. However, through his research of soybean oil, Julian found a substitute for expensive sterols. By 1950 he perfected a method that eventually lowered the cost of sterols to fewer than 20 cents a gram. Julian's discovery ultimately enabled millions of people suffering from arthritis to obtain relief through the use of cortisone, a sterol derivative. In 1953 Julian founded his own company, Julian

Institute in Franklin Park, Illinois, and then another one in Mexico. The Institute produced mainly sterols. Then in 1961, Julian sold his institute to Smith, Klein, and French for several million dollars. In honor of Dr. Percy Julian, the chemistry and mathematics building at De Paw University is named for him.

In addition to the inventions of African American men, African American women have also contributed to society with their inventions. Sarah Breedlowe Walker, known as Madam C. J. Walker, was such a woman. Born in 1867 from ex-slaves and passing away in 1919, Walker was one of the first white or black American women to become a self-made millionairess. Walker was orphaned by the age of six years, married at age fourteen years, and widowed by age twenty years. Walker and her daughter, Lelia, moved to Saint Louis where Walker did laundry for an income. Walker noticed that her hair was falling out, so she experimented with products, but nothing worked. Then she said a black man came to her in a dream and gave her a secret formula for growing hair. Then in 1905 she moved to Denver where she net and married C. J. Walker. Her second husband helped her advertise and promote a product called Madam C. J. Walker's Hair Grower. Her marriage to her second husband did not last, but she continued to develop more hair care products including softeners and conditioners until she eventually created an entire Walker System of hair care. She set up a manufacturing company from her original hair-care system. She later expanded her products to an entire line of cosmetics for African American women. Within a few years, Walker's company was paying over $200,000 annually to its personnel including a school to train salespeople.

Garrett Morgan's inventions greatly contributed to public safety. His invention which led to the gas mask saved many lives in wars and in firemen's work. His automatic traffic light made possible the organized system of vehicle traffic. Another inventor, Dr. Percy Julian, contributed to the medical field by creating derivative drugs to ease the suffering of people with certain medical problems, especially to average people who could not otherwise afford the former extremely high costs of certain drugs. Moreover, Madam C. J. Walker made contributions to women's hair and cosmetic needs by developing a hair-growing formula and an array of hair softeners and conditioners, and cosmetics for African American women. Thus, many African American inventors have greatly contributed to the constructive advancement of society.

Process

Process

A **process** essay tells the reader **how something is done** step by step, like baking a cake or changing a tire on a car. A process essay is a "how to" essay. Generally, each time you begin writing about another step in the process, start a new paragraph.

Outline

(Process)

How To Find Major Points

I. Questions
    A. Title of chapter
    B. Sub-headings

II. Words in special type
    A. Boldface
    B. Italics

III. Key words
    A. Details
    B. Numbers

IV. Arrangement of information
    A. Comparison/Contrast
    B. Cause and Effect
    C. Process
    D. Argumentation
    E. Classification and Division
    F. Description
    G. Definition
    H. Exemplification
    I. Narration

Process – Essay

Identifying Main points When Reading A Textbook

Being a student requires much reading. Oftentimes chapters in textbooks are very long and contain much information. The student is required to determine and understand what information is most important. Asking questions, identifying words in special type, noticing key words, and determining the arrangement of the information when reading textbooks will enable a student to find the major points.

Most chapters in textbooks have titles, and the title usually contains the topic that the author will discuss in that chapter. The first step in searching for major points is to turn the title into a question. Begin the question with the word, "who, what, why, when, where" or "how". Sometimes words in the title will need to be rearranged. When reading, look for the answers to the question that the title has become. Those answers will be the major points in the chapter. Many times the sub-headings will answer the question that the title asks. The sub-headings can also be turned into questions, and the answers to those questions will be the most important material in the chapter.

Another clue to discover major points is special type. Look for words that are printed in boldface type or italics. Authors put certain words into special print because the writers want the reader to pay special attention to these words because the special words are important to understanding the information being explained. The definitions of words printed in special type are usually included in the same sentences as the notable words, and these words are many times connected with the major points.

Furthermore, key words can direct a reader to the most important information in a chapter. Most paragraphs are written deductively – the general statement first followed by details. Examples are one form of details. The reader should look for the words, "for example, for instance, to illustrate" and "such as" and then go to the sentence right before these words. That sentence will usually contain a major point. Numbers such as "first, second" and other signal words like "finally, lastly" indicate that the author is listing items. Each item on the list in the information is a major point.

Finally, the reader should analyze and decide which rhetorical pattern or arrangement of the information the author is using. The author may be comparing and/or contrasting two people or items in which case each similarity and difference is a major point. If the author is writing about causes and effects, each cause and each effect is a major point. However, a process explains to the reader how to accomplish a task step by step. Each step in the process is a major point. Another rhetorical pattern is argumentation in which two sides of an issue are debated, and the author tries to persuade the reader to agree with him or her. Each reason the author presents to defend his or her side of the argument is a major point. Still, information can be classified and divided. An author could write about three different types of films, such as musicals, comedies, and science fiction, categorizing them into different groups. The type of each group and the characteristics of each group are major points.

In conclusion, to select the most important information when reading a chapter in a textbook, a reader should first turn the title of the chapter and sub-headings into questions and look for the answers to those questions. A reader should also search for clues like words in specialized print type and signal words that point to the most important information in a chapter. These steps along with discovering how the written material is arranged will help a reader to select the most important information when reading a textbook.

Comparison
and
Contrast

Comparison and Contrast

Compare means how two people or two things are the **same**. **Contrast** means how two people or two things are **different**. Whether your essay only compares, only contrasts, or compares *and* contrasts, both subjects compared and/or contrasted in your essay should have something in common, for example: two teachers, two department stores, two retail discount stores, two movies (two westerns, two comedies, two science fiction), two politicians, two singers, two character traits or emotions that can be confused (courage and recklessness, love and infatuation), two dates, two employers.

There are **two ways to organize your information** in a comparison and contrast essay. One way is to write everything you want to write about subject number one. Then in the second half of your essay, write everything you want to write about subject number two. This method is called **subject by subject** or **block form**. The second way to organize your information is to discuss both subjects together with regards to each similarity and/or each difference. This method is called **point by point**.

Outline
(Comparison and Contrast)

Subject by Subject
or
Block Form

History Repeats Itself
President Lincoln and President Kennedy

I. President Abraham Lincoln
- A. Election – 1860
- B. Civil Rights concerns
- C. Lost child while living in White House – William Lincoln
- D. Assassinated
    1. Shot in head
    2. Shot on a Friday
    3. Shot in presence of wife
- E. Successor – Andrew Johnson
    1. Same last name
    2. Born 1808
    3. Southern Democrat
    4. Seat in Senate
- F. Secretary
    1. Secretary Kennedy
    2. Warned Lincoln not to go to theater where Lincoln was shot
- G. Assassin – John Wilkes Booth
    1. Born 1839
    2. Assassinated before going to trial
    3. From theater to warehouse
- H. Numbers of letters in names
    1. Lincoln – seven letters
    2. Andrew Johnson – thirteen letters
    3. John Wilkes Booth – fifteen letters

II. President John Kennedy
- A. Election – 1960
- B. Civil Rights concerns
- C. Lost child while living in White House – Patrick Kennedy
- D. Assassinated
    1. Shot in head
    2. Shot on a Friday
    3. Shot in presence of wife
- E. Successor – Lyndon Johnson
    1. Same last name
    2. Born 1908
    3. Southern Democrat
    4. Seat in Senate
- F. Secretary
    1. Secretary Lincoln
    2. Warned Kennedy not to go to Dallas where Kennedy was shot
- G. Alleged assassin – Lee Harvey Oswald
    1. Born 1939
    2. Assassinated before going to trial
    3. From warehouse to theater
- H. Numbers of letters in names
    1. Kennedy – seven letters
    2. Lyndon Johnson – thirteen letters
    3. Lee Harvey Oswald – fifteen letters

Comparison/Contrast – Essay
(Subject by Subject or Block Form)

History Repeats Itself

Upon studying history, a person will discover that throughout time, similar events occur but with different people involved. This phenomenon includes various leaders of countries. Several similarities of the lives and times of two presidents of the United States, Abraham Lincoln and John F. Kennedy, prove that sometimes history does repeat itself.

First of all, President Lincoln was elected to the presidency in 1860. He was the Republican candidate who received 180 electoral votes against his opponents: National Democrat John C. Breckinridge who received 72 electoral votes, followed by Constitutional Unionist John Bell receiving 39 electoral votes, and Democrat Stephen A. Douglas receiving 12 electoral votes.

Next, during President Lincoln's administration, he was concerned with Civil Rights issues. Lincoln detested slavery. He believed that people of African descent under the United States government were entitled to all of the natural rights enumerated in the Declaration of Independence – the rights to life, liberty, and the pursuit of happiness. As the American Civil War raged on, Lincoln issued the Emancipation Proclamation freeing all people of African descent who were being held as slaves in Southern States that had seceded from the Union. Lincoln worked diligently to permanently end slavery throughout the entire United States and persistently shepherded the 13th Amendment to the United States Constitution through Congress to achieve his commitment. Upon visiting the newly captured capital of the Confederacy, Richmond, Virginia, as President Lincoln and his entourage walked through the streets of rubble, Lincoln encountered an elderly African American man who had been just freed from slavery. When the elderly man saw Lincoln, he bowed to Lincoln, and Lincoln bowed back to him. In Lincoln's last speech which took place three days before he was fatally shot, he called for giving African American men (no women could vote then) the right to vote, calling that right as a first step with other steps to follow.

President Lincoln and his wife, Mary Todd Lincoln, lost a child through death while living in the White House. President and Mrs. Lincoln had four sons together – Robert Todd Lincoln, born in 1843; Edward Baker Lincoln, born in 1846; William 'Willie" Wallace Lincoln, born in 1850; and Thomas 'Tad' Lincoln, born in 1853. During Lincoln's presidency from March 1861 to April 1865, President and Mrs. Lincoln's son, Willie, died at eleven years of age of an acute malarial infection in 1862.

In addition, President Lincoln was assassinated by being shot in the head on a Friday and in the presence of his wife. On Good Friday, April 14, 1865, President and Mrs. Lincoln, and their guests, Major Henry Rathbone and his step-sister and fiancée, Miss Clara Harris, were sitting in the presidential box at Ford's Theatre in Washington, D.C., watching the play, *Our American Cousin*. At approximately 10:15 p.m., an actor named John Wilkes Booth entered the presidential box from behind President Lincoln and shot Lincoln in the back of the head at close range with a derringer. The bullet entered Lincoln's head behind his left ear and traveled crosswise through Lincoln's brain and came to rest behind his right eye. Moments later, doctors who were in the audience reached the president, laid him onto the floor and revived him. They then carried him across the street and into Petersen's Boarding House where they laid his six-foot, four-inch frame diagonally across a bed. The doctors knew that Lincoln's wound was mortal, but during the night they did what they could to keep him alive. Abraham Lincoln passed away at 7:22 the following morning, on April 15, 1865, without ever regaining consciousness. After President Lincoln had passed away, his successor was Andrew Johnson. Born in 1808 in Raleigh, North Carolina, Johnson had been a Southern Democrat who was a United States Senator of Tennessee from 1857 to 1862.

Also, Abraham Lincoln had a secretary whose last name was Kennedy. Secretary Kennedy advised President Lincoln not to go to the theater where Lincoln was assassinated.

John Wilkes Booth, born in 1839, assassinated President Lincoln in Ford's Theatre in Washington, D.C., and escaped on horseback. Booth was caught in a tobacco barn on a farm near Bowling Green, Virginia, nearly 60 miles away from Washington, D.C. on April 26, 1865. After the barn was surrounded by federal troops, the co-conspirator who was traveling with Booth, surrendered. When Booth refused to surrender, the barn was set on fire. A soldier named Boston Corbett later claimed to have shot Booth. Booth was mortally shot and was dragged from the barn and onto the porch of the farmhouse where he died 2½ hours later.

The name "Lincoln" has 7 letters in it. Lincoln's successor's name, "Andrew Johnson," contains 13 letters, whereas Lincoln's assassin's name, "John Wilkes Booth," has 15 letters in it.

Exactly 100 years after President Lincoln was elected president, Democrat John F. Kennedy was elected to the presidency in 1960, receiving 303 electoral votes followed by his Republican opponent, Richard Nixon, who received 219 electoral votes, and non-party candidate, Senator Harry F. Byrd, who received 15 electoral votes.

Like Lincoln, President John F. Kennedy responded to Civil Rights for African Americans. Kennedy ordered an end to discrimination in housing owned, operated, or financed by the federal government; established the President's Committee on Equal Employment Opportunity; and appointed numerous African Americans to prominent federal positions. Kennedy also called for desegregation of public facilities and greater authority for the attorney general in bringing suits against segregated school systems.

Similar to President and Mrs. Lincoln, John F. Kennedy and his wife, Jacqueline Kennedy, lost a child through death while occupying the White House. President Kennedy and his wife, Jacqueline Kennedy, had a daughter, Caroline Kennedy, who was born in 1957, and John F. Kennedy, Jr., who was born in 1960. During Kennedy's presidency from January 1961 to November 1963, President and Mrs. Kennedy had a son, Patrick Bouvier Kennedy, who was born on August 9, 1963, and died 39 hours later after being born 5½ weeks prematurely. Patrick's premature birth caused him to have a respiratory problem which caused him to have trouble with breathing; the breathing problem was too much for his heart.

Like Lincoln, President Kennedy was assassinated by being shot in the head, on a Friday, and in the company of his wife. On Friday, November 22, 1963, President John F. Kennedy was traveling in an open limousine in a motorcade moving through the streets of Dallas, Texas, enroute to the Dallas Trade Mart for a scheduled luncheon address. His wife, Jacqueline Kennedy, sat next to him on his left side, and Texas Governor John Connally sat in the seat directly in front of the President. Mrs. Connally sat on her husband's left side. Two United States secret service agents sat in the front seat, one behind the steering wheel driving the limousine, and the other agent sat on the passenger side. Thick, enthusiastic crowds lined the streets to see the President pass by on the sunny, warm day. At approximately 12:30 p.m., 3 or 4 shots rang out! Three bullets came from behind the President from the sixth floor of the Texas School Book Depository. One bullet struck President Kennedy near the base of his neck exiting through his throat. Then another bullet slammed into President Kennedy's head, sending blood, brain matter, and bone fragments high into the air. A large portion of the right side of his head had been torn away. Kennedy was rushed to Parkland Memorial Hospital where emergency room doctors enlarged the wound in his throat in an attempt to permit him to breathe better, gave him transfusions of whole blood, and tried to stimulate his heart with chest massage, but his head wound was fatal. At 1:33 p.m., a press aide announced that President Kennedy had passed away.

John Kennedy's successor was Lyndon Johnson. Johnson was born in 1908 on the Pedernales River between Stonewall and Johnson City, Texas. He was also a Democrat and had served as a United States Senator of Texas from 1949 to 1961.

President Kennedy had a secretary named Lincoln. Secretary Lincoln warned President Kennedy not to go to Dallas where Kennedy ended up being assassinated.

According to the Warren Commission appointed by President Lyndon Johnson to investigate the assassination of President Kennedy, President Kennedy was assassinated by Lee Harvey Oswald who was born in 1939, exactly 100 years after John Wilkes Booth. Oswald shot Kennedy from a book depository building and ran to the Texas Theatre where he was captured by police 45 minutes later. On November 24, 1963, Oswald was shot and killed by a Dallas nightclub owner, Jack Ruby, as Oswald was being transferred to the county jail.

Like President Lincoln's last name, the name "Kennedy" contains 7 letters. The name "Lyndon Johnson" contains 13 letters as does the name, "Andrew Johnson". The name "Lee Harvey Oswald" like the name "John Wilkes Booth," contains 15 letters.

In conclusion, there are many similarities between President Lincoln and President Kennedy and circumstances in their lives. There is exactly a 100-year time span between the presidents' elections, their successors' births, and assassins' births. During their administrations, both presidents were exceptionally concerned with Civil Rights, and, with their wives, lost children through death while living in the White House. Both presidents were fatally shot in the head, on a Friday, and in the company of their wives. Their successors, who shared the same last name, were former Senators from the same part of the country and belonged to the same political party. Both assassins either fired their guns or escaped to a warehouse and theater, and were killed before standing trial for being accused of killing the presidents. Each pair of presidents, successors, and assassins contains the same number of letters in their names. Thus, history does sometimes repeat itself.

Outline
(Comparison and Contrast)

Point by Point

History Repeats Itself
President Lincoln and President Kennedy

I. Election 100 years apart
   A. Lincoln – 1860
   B. Kennedy – 1960

II. Civil Rights concerns
   A. Lincoln
   B. Kennedy

III. Presidents and wives lost children while living in White House
   A. William Lincoln
   B. Patrick Kennedy

IV. Assassination
   A. Lincoln
      1. Shot in head
      2. Shot on a Friday
      3. Shot in presence of wife
   B. Kennedy
      1. Shot in head
      2. Shot on a Friday
      3. Shot in presence of wife

V. Successors
   A. Andrew Johnson
      1. Same last name
      2. Born 1808
      3. Southern Democrat
      4. Seat in Senate
   B. Lyndon Johnson
      1. Same last name
      2. Born 1908
      3. Southern Democrat
      4. Seat in Senate

VI. Secretaries
   A. President Lincoln
      1. Secretary – Kennedy
      2. Warned President Lincoln not to go to theater
   B. President Kennedy
      1. Secretary – Lincoln
      2. Warned President Kennedy not to go to Dallas

VII. Assassins
   A. John Wilkes Booth
      1. Born 1839
      2. Assassinated before going to trial
      3. From theater to warehouse
   B. Lee Harvey Oswald
      1. Born 1939
      2. Assassinated before going to trial
      3. From warehouse to theater

VIII. Numbers of letters in names
   A. Presidents – seven letters
      1. Lincoln
      2. Kennedy
   B. Successors – thirteen letters
      1. Andrew Johnson
      2. Lyndon Johnson
   C. Assassins – fifteen letters
      1. John Wilkes Booth
      2. Lee Harvey Oswald

Comparison/Contrast – Essay
(Point by Point)

History Repeats Itself

Upon studying history, a person will discover that throughout time, similar events occur but with different people involved. This phenomenon includes various leaders of countries. Several similarities of the lives and times of two presidents of the United States, Abraham Lincoln and John F. Kennedy, prove that sometimes history does repeat itself.

Specifically, President Lincoln and President Kennedy were elected to the presidency exactly 100 years apart. Lincoln, the Republican candidate, was elected in 1860, receiving 180 electoral votes against his opponents: National Democrat John C. Breckinridge who received 72 electoral votes, followed by Constitutional Unionist John Bell receiving 39 electoral votes, and Democrat Stephen A. Douglas receiving 12 electoral votes. One hundred years later, in 1960, Democrat John F. Kennedy was elected president by receiving 303 electoral votes followed by his Republican opponent, Richard M. Nixon, who received 219 electoral votes, and non-party candidate, Senator Harry F. Byrd, who received 15 electoral votes.

During their administrations, both President Lincoln and President Kennedy were concerned with Civil Rights issues. Lincoln detested slavery. He believed that people of African descent under the Untied States government were entitled to all of the natural rights enumerated in the Declaration of Independence – the rights to life, liberty, and the pursuit of happiness. As the American Civil War raged on, Lincoln issued the Emancipation Proclamation freeing all people of African descent who were being held as slaves in Southern states that had seceded from the Union. Lincoln worked diligently to permanently end slavery throughout the entire United States and persistently shepherded the 13th amendment to the United States Constitution to achieve his commitment. Upon visiting the newly captured capital of the Confederacy, Richmond, Virginia, as President Lincoln and his entourage walked through the streets of rubble, Lincoln encountered an elderly African American man who had been just freed from slavery. When the elderly man saw Lincoln, he bowed, and Lincoln bowed back to him. In Lincoln's last speech which took place three days before he was fatally shot, he called for giving African American men (women could not vote then) the right to vote, calling that right as a first step with other steps to follow. Likewise, President Kennedy responded to Civil Rights for African Americans by ordering an end to discrimination in housing owned, operated, or financed by the federal government; established the President's Committee on Equal Employment Opportunity; and appointed numerous African Americans to prominent federal positions. Kennedy also called for desegregation of public facilities and greater authority for the attorney general in bringing suits against segregated school systems.

Personally, both presidents and their wives lost children through death while living in the White House. Abraham Lincoln and his wife, Mary Todd Lincoln, had 4 sons together: Robert Todd Lincoln, born in 1843; Edward Baker Lincoln, born in 1846; William 'Willie' Wallace Lincoln, born in 1850; and Thomas 'Tad' Lincoln, born in 1853. During Lincoln's presidency from March 1861 to April 1865, President and Mrs. Lincoln's son, Willie, died at 11 years of age of an acute malarial infection in 1862. Similarly, the Kennedys were parents of young children while occupying the White House. President Kennedy and his wife, Jacqueline Kennedy, had a daughter, Caroline Kennedy, who was born in 1957, and John F. Kennedy, Jr., who was born in 1960. During Kennedy's presidency from January 1961 to November 1963, President and Mrs. Kennedy had a son, Patrick Bouvier Kennedy, who was born on August 9, 1963, and died 39 hours later after being born 5½ weeks prematurely. Patrick's premature birth caused him to have a respiratory problem which caused him to have trouble with breathing; the breathing problem was too much for his heart.

Also, President Lincoln and President Kennedy were both assassinated by being shot in the head on a Friday and in the presence of their wives. On Good Friday, April 14, 1865, President and Mrs. Lincoln, and their guests, Major Henry Rathbone and his step-sister and fiancée, Miss Clara Harris, were sitting in the presidential box at Ford's Theatre in Washington, D.C., watching the play, *Our American Cousin*. At approximately 10:15 P.M., an actor named John Wilkes Booth entered the presidential box from behind President Lincoln and shot Lincoln in the back of the head at close range with a derringer. The bullet entered Lincoln's head behind his left ear and traveled crosswise through Lincoln's brain and came to rest behind his right eye. Moments later, doctors who were in the audience reached the president, laid him onto the floor, and revived him. They then carried him across the street and into Petersen's Boarding House where they laid his six-foot, four-inch frame diagonally across a bed. The doctors knew that Lincoln's wound was mortal, but during the night they did what they could to keep him alive. Abraham Lincoln passed away at 7:22 the following morning, on April 15, 1865, without ever regaining consciousness. Likewise, on Friday, November 22, 1963, President John F. Kennedy was traveling in an open limousine in a motorcade moving through the streets of Dallas, Texas, enroute to the Dallas Trade Mart for a scheduled luncheon address. His wife, Jacqueline Kennedy, sat next to him on his left side, and Texas Governor John Connally sat in the seat directly in front of the President. Mrs. Connally sat on her husband's left side. Two United States secret service agents sat in the front seat, one behind the steering wheel driving the limousine, and the other agent sat on the passenger side. Thick, enthusiastic crowds lined the streets to see the President pass by on the sunny, warm day. At approximately 12:30 P.M., 3 or 4 shots rang out! Three bullets came from behind the president from the sixth floor of the Texas School Book Depository. One bullet struck President Kennedy near the base of his neck exiting through his throat. Then another bullet slammed into President Kennedy's head, sending blood, brain matter, and bone fragments high into the air. A large portion of the right side of his head had been torn away. Kennedy was rushed to Parkland Memorial Hospital where emergency room doctors enlarged the wound in his throat in an attempt to permit him to breathe better, gave him transfusions of whole blood, and tried to stimulate his heart with chest massage, but his head wound was fatal. At 1:33 P.M., a press aide announced that President Kennedy had passed away.

Both successors had the same last name, were born exactly 100 years apart, were Southern Democrats, and held seats in the Senate. Abraham Lincoln's successor was Andrew Johnson who was born in 1808 in Raleigh, North Carolina. He was a Democrat who served as a United States Senator of Tennessee from 1857 to 1862. John Kennedy's successor was Lyndon Johnson who was born in 1908 on the Pedernales River between Stonewall and Johnson City, Texas. He was also a Democrat and served as a United States Senator of Texas from 1949 to 1961.

55

Furthermore, the secretaries of President Lincoln and President Kennedy warned the presidents not to go to the places where each president ended up being assassinated. President Lincoln' secretary whose name was Kennedy advised President Lincoln not to go to the theater where Lincoln was fatally shot. Similarly, President Kennedy's secretary whose name was Lincoln advised President Kennedy not to go to Dallas, Texas, where Kennedy ended up being killed.

The assassins of President Lincoln and President Kennedy were born exactly 100 years apart, themselves killed before going to trial, and occupied a theater and a warehouse during or after the shootings of the two presidents. John Wilkes Booth, who was born in 1839, shot Lincoln in Ford's Theatre in Washington, D.C., and escaped on horseback. He was caught in a tobacco barn on a farm near Bowling Green, Virginia, nearly 60 miles away from Washington, D.C., on April 26, 1865. After the barn was surrounded by federal troops, the co-conspirator who was traveling with Booth, surrendered. When Booth refused to surrender, the barn was set on fire. A soldier named Boston Corbett later claimed to have shot Booth. Booth was mortally shot and was dragged from the barn and onto the porch of the farmhouse where he died 2½ hours later. Likewise, according to the Warren Commission appointed by President Lyndon Johnson to investigate the assassination of President Kennedy, President Kennedy was assassinated by Lee Harvey Oswald who was born in 1939. Oswald shot Kennedy from a book depository building and ran to the Texas Theatre where he was captured by police 45 minutes later. On November 24, 1963, Oswald was shot and killed by a Dallas nightclub owner, Jack Ruby, as Oswald was being transferred to the county jail.

Lastly, each pair of presidents, successors, and assassins have the same number of letters in their names. The names "Lincoln" and "Kennedy" both contain 7 letters; the names "Andrew Johnson" and "Lyndon Johnson" each contain 13 letters; and the names "John Wilkes Booth" and "Lee Harvey Oswald" each contain 15 letters.

In conclusion, there are many similarities between President Lincoln and President Kennedy and circumstances in their lives. There is exactly a 100-year time span between the presidents' elections, their successors' births, and assassins' births. During their administrations, both presidents were exceptionally concerned with Civil Rights, and, with their wives, lost children through death while living in the White House. Both presidents were fatally shot in the head, on a Friday, and in the company of their wives. Their successors, who shared the same last name, were former Senators from the same part of the country and belonged to the same political party. Both assassins either fired their guns or escaped to a warehouse and theater, and were killed before standing trial for being accused of killing the presidents. Each pair of presidents, successors, and assassins contains the same number of letters in their names. Thus, history does sometimes repeat itself.

Classification

Classification

The classification pattern can be thought of as an extended comparison/contrast format. The key word in writing a classification essay is **types** – types of people or things. The topic of the essay should be subdivided into three categories or groups. For example:

Topic: Drivers

Categories: Excellent drivers
Average drivers
Poor drivers

Examining individual drivers within a group, such as excellent drivers, is comparing them. How are these drivers the same? Common characteristics of the other two groups, such as average drivers, and poor drivers, should also be considered.

Examining the group of excellent drivers as a whole, against the other two groups, average drivers and poor drivers, is contrasting. How is the group of excellent drivers different from the group of average drivers and the group of poor drivers? How are average drivers different from excellent drivers and poor drivers? Finally, how are poor drivers different from excellent drivers and average drivers?

Outline
(Classification)

Drivers on the Road

I. Excellent drivers
  A. Traffic laws
  B. Alertness
  C. Courtesy

II. Average drivers
  A. Traffic laws
  B. Alertness
  C. Courtesy
III. Poor drivers
  A. Traffic laws
  B. Alertness
  C. Courtesy

Note: This outline is written in **parallel structure**. (Notice the words after A, B, and C are the same.)

Drivers on the Road

Most people in the United States drive cars, vans, or pickup trucks. With many motor vehicles simultaneous on the road, drivers are forced to interact with the driving actions of other people. Sharing the road with excellent drivers is safer than coping with average and poor drivers.

Excellent drivers consistently follow traffic laws and are alert and courteous. These drivers stay within the speed limits which are predetermined to be safe speeds and reach the maximum allowed speed limit only when passing other cars, which they pass on the left side. They consistently obey the signals of traffic lights and all signs such as stop, school zone, and turning-lane signs. Excellent drivers do not cross over double yellow lines on the road. These drivers concentrate on their driving and the driving of other motorists. In addition to primarily looking at the road before them, their eyes frequently dart among the rearview and side mirrors, ready to react to a sudden, dangerous maneuver of another driver. They exercise active listening skills to hear sirens of emergency vehicles. Upon hearing a siren, excellent drivers pull over to the curb lane and stop until the police car, ambulance, or fire truck passes by them. These drivers are courteous to other drivers by slowing their speeds to let other cars merge into on-going traffic on highways. When a confusing situation of two stationary cars arises and it is unclear as to which driver should start first, the paramount driver will wave to the other driver to let the other driver continue onward.

Although excellent drivers uniformly excel in admirable driving habits, average drivers are less scrupulous in performing good driving practices. Average drivers usually comply with traffic laws, are alert most of the time, and are occasionally polite to other motorists. Most of the time average drivers obey traffic laws but may sometimes take unsafe risks occasionally exceeding the speed limit and sometimes passing another car on the right side. Moreover, at times they will drive through a yellow, caution traffic light which may cause an accident if another driver starts to pass through an intersection too soon. Average drivers are usually alert to their driving and the driving of others, but occasionally let themselves become distracted by looking at scenery, manipulating the car radio controls, or conversing with another person over a telephone while driving. During occasional, brief periods of inattentiveness, an average driver may not see a dangerous situation ahead in time to avoid it. Even though courtesy is among the positive attributes of average drivers, they may not use the cars' turn signals for a sufficient length of time before crossing over into a lane in front of another car by letting the turn signal light blink only two or three times before switching lanes. Sometimes average drivers will not bring their cars to a complete stop at a four-way-stop intersection before proceeding forward.

Although any driver can make a mistake in driving, poor drivers are the most hazardous of all types of drivers. Poor drivers seem to be oblivious to all other drivers, cars, and pedestrians. An atrocious driver will pull out in front of a moving car when the moving car is very close to the bad driver's car, and then the poor driver will proceed very slowly. When dreadful drivers approach caution lights that are ready to turn red signaling drivers to stop, bad drivers will suddenly accelerate the speeds of their vehicles and zoom through intersections at unsafe, fast speeds. Poor drivers may also disobey red lights and stop signs which increase the possibility of accidents. Bad drivers frequently exceed speed limits and travel at excessive rates of speed during unsafe road conditions such as rain and snow-covered road surfaces. Poor drivers are not alert and attentive when driving. They look at the road ahead of them and at scenery on both sides of their vehicles without frequently looking at the rearview and side mirrors. Therefore, they are unaware of what other motorists are doing around them such as passing them. These unsafe drivers are many times unaware of approaching emergency vehicles such as ambulances, fire trucks, and police cars because they are not using the cars' mirrors and may have the car radio volume so loud that they cannot hear sirens, or in the case of some elderly drivers, may have partial hearing loss. When poor drivers sight an emergency vehicle, they may continue traveling instead of pulling over to the curb lane and stopping until the emergency vehicle has passed. Atrocious drivers exercise little or no courtesy. For example, another motorist is traveling in the curb lane while employing a left turn signal to switch to the left lane. Poor drivers who are a few car lengths behind in the left lane will increase their speeds and pass the other motorist instead of letting the other motorist switch to the left lane while the poor drivers are still a few car lengths behind the other driver. Poor motorists make turns without using turn signals and may not turn on headlights and taillights at dusk, making their cars less visible to other drivers.

Poor drivers are unobservant of traffic laws, inattentive to their driving, and discourteous to other drivers, making poor drivers the most dangerous motorists on roads. Average drivers basically follow traffic regulations, but their occasional risks make them potentially hazardous to other drivers at times. Therefore, excellent drivers who consistently comply with traffic laws to the best of their abilities and are vigilant and courteous to other drivers are the safest drivers with which to share roads.

Cause
and
Effect

Cause and Effect

A **cause and effect essay** discusses the causes and/or effects of an action or event.
A **cause** is a **reason** for something happening. An **effect** is a **result** of something.
Generally, each cause and each effect will be a separate paragraph in the essay.

Read diagrams from left to right.

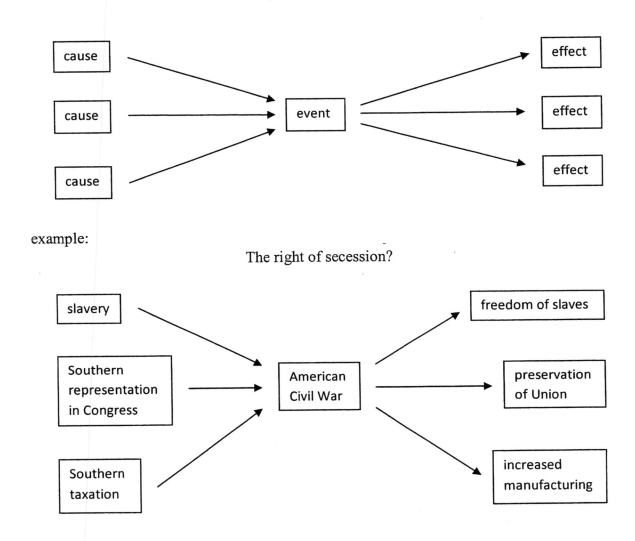

example:

The right of secession?

Sometimes the event can be used as a cause or an effect.

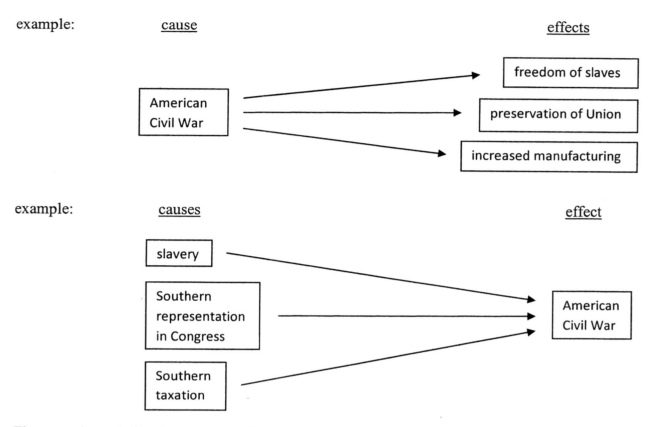

There can be a chain of causes and effects.

example:

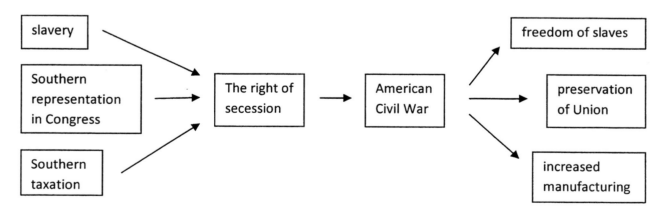

Slavery, Southern representation in Congress, and Southern taxation are the causes. The effect of those causes is the right of secession. Do some states have the right to leave the United States and form their own country? Then the right of secession becomes a cause for the effect – the American Civil War. Then the American Civil War becomes a cause for the effects – freedom of slaves, preservation of the Union, and increased manufacturing.

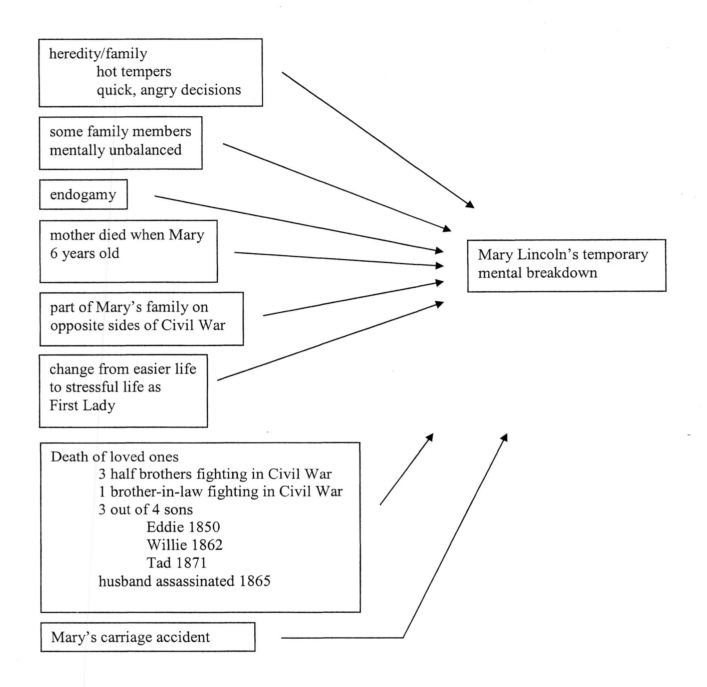

heredity/family
        hot tempers
        quick, angry decisions

some family members
mentally unbalanced

endogamy

mother died when Mary
6 years old

part of Mary's family on
opposite sides of Civil War

change from easier life
to stressful life as
First Lady

Mary Lincoln's temporary
mental breakdown

Death of loved ones
        3 half brothers fighting in Civil War
        1 brother-in-law fighting in Civil War
        3 out of 4 sons
                Eddie 1850
                Willie 1862
                Tad 1871
        husband assassinated 1865

Mary's carriage accident

Outline

(Cause and Effect)

Mary Lincoln's Tragedies

I. Heredity
   A. hot tempers
   B. quick, angry decisions
   C. some family members mentally unbalanced
   D. endogamy

II. Lifestyle
   A. popular before First Lady
   B. as First Lady and after, publicly criticized

III. Death of loved ones
   A. mother
   B. three half brothers fighting in Civil War
   C. one brother-in-law fighting in Civil War
   D. three sons
   E. husband assassinated

IV. Carriage accident
   A. head injury
   B. 1863
   C. hospitalized and incapacitated for three weeks

V. Temporary mental breakdown
   A. judged legally insane from May 1875 to June 1876
   B. four months in private sanitorium

special note – Most of these incidences happened within a period of ten years.

Alternate Outline (IF there were two or more effects)
(Cause and Effect)

Mary Lincoln's Tragedies

Thesis statement: Heredity, a change in public reaction towards her, death of loved ones, and a carriage accident probably led to Mary Lincoln's temporary insanity.

I. Causes
   A. heredity
      1. hot tempers
      2. quick, angry decisions
      3. some family members mentally unbalanced
      4. endogamy

   B. lifestyle
      1. popular before First Lady
      2. as First Lady and after, publicly criticized

   C. death of loved ones
      1. mother
      2. three half brothers fighting in Civil War
      3. one brother-in-law fighting in Civil War
      4. three sons
      5. husband assassinated

   D. Carriage accident
      1. head injury
      2. 1863
      3. hospitalized and incapacitated for three weeks

II. Effect
   A. temporary mental breakdown
      1. judged legally insane from May 1875 to June 1876
      2. four months in private sanitarium

In an outline, if you have an "A", you should have at least a "B". If you have a number "1", you should have at least a number "2". Because this topic has only one effect, this outline may not be suitable. Therefore, the first outline may be more suitable for this topic.

Mary Lincoln's Tragedies

Mary Lincoln's life was full of beautiful, happy times and several tragedies. She was the wife of America's sixteenth president, Abraham Lincoln, who served as the nation's chief executive from March 4, 1961 to April 15, 1865. President Lincoln was assassinated while serving as president during his second term in office. Later in Mary Lincoln's life, she was judged legally insane in May 1875 until June 1876. She spent four months of that one year in a private sanitorium. After she was judged "competent to conduct her own affairs," her letters reveal a remarkably keen mind. She also made several excursions to France and Italy. Heredity, a change in public reaction towards her, death of loved ones, and a carriage accident probably led to Mary Lincoln's temporary insanity.

Heredity could have caused a tendency towards mental illness in Mary Lincoln. Born Mary Todd, Mary Lincoln came from a large family which consisted of a father, mother, step-mother, and fifteen brothers and sisters. The Todd family in Kentucky, Illinois, and elsewhere had a long, established record for quick angry decisions and contained proportionately more than its share of mentally unbalanced members. Also, the Todd family members were aristocrats, and the family members knew it. Abraham Lincoln once said that God is satisfied with one "D" in His name, but the Todds think they need two "Ds" in their name. The self-important perception that members of the Todd family had of themselves is probably the reason that there were many intermarriages in the Todd family. For example, Mary Lincoln's parents were cousins. Endogamy, or genetically related couples producing offspring, may have affected Mary Lincoln since sometimes endogamy produces innate flaws or weaknesses in people.

Another possible reason that led to Mary Lincoln's mental breakdown was the change in the public's reactions to her. During her young adult years, she enjoyed a popular life in high society. She was an expert on the social graces, intelligent, and interested in politics. She was considered to be one of the most eligible, marriageable young women in Lexington, Kentucky. Her father, who was a banker, was a well-known citizen and had many influential friends. While growing up, seeing people in her father's house like the Great Compromiser, Statesman Henry Clay, was commonplace to her. Before she dated Lincoln, she was romantically pursued by Patrick Henry's grandson. She dated the prominent Judge Stephen Douglas who became Lincoln's chief political rival, including one of Lincoln's opponents in the 1860 presidential election. After enjoying a popular, young adulthood, years later in 1861 when she became the First Lady, she experienced a stressful change in the public's reaction to her. Her emotional outbursts like the time she emotionally exploded at General Grant's wife were seen as unfavorable to the public. She was viciously attacked in Washington, D.C. newspapers and by other individuals. Like many families at that time, members of Mary Lincoln's family were divided on loyalties. Of the family members who lived to adulthood, six were Union loyalists and eight took the Confederate side. Her Union patriotism was publicly questioned many times. At one point, she was accused of being a Confederate spy. She suffered much stress from the general public's perception of her from her beginning role as First Lady in 1861 to her death in July 1882.

Moreover, death took from Mary Lincoln most of the people who were closest to her and most cherished. Her mother died when Mary was six years of age. As an adult, three of Mary Lincoln's half-brothers and one brother-in-law were killed fighting in the Civil War between 1861 and 1865. Three of her four dearly loved children died before reaching adulthood: Eddie in 1850, age nearly four years died of "consumption"; Willie in 1862 (in the White House) at age eleven years, from an acute malarial infection; and Tad in 1871 at eighteen years of age from pleurisy. Her cherished husband was violently gunned down in 1865 as she sat beside him.

In addition to the loss of loved ones, during the battle of Gettysburg, Pennsylvania, in 1863, Mary Lincoln was violently thrown from her carriage while en route to the White House from the Soldiers' Home. She received a serious head injury when her head hit a sharp rock as she hit the ground. She was hospitalized and incapacitated for three weeks.

In conclusion, Mary Todd Lincoln came from a family that contained some mentally disturbed members, and her parents were cousins. The change from growing up in a prestigious environment and then being savagely criticized by Washington, D.C. socialites, politicians and their wives, and the general public caused her much stress. During her lifetime, she lost several people through passing away, some of whom were her closest loved ones. She also suffered a serious head injury when she was the First Lady. Most of these tragedies occurred within a period of ten years. The Todd family weakness of mental disorders most likely created a natural weakness in Mary Lincoln to begin with, and her distressful situations and tragedies no doubt furthered this, leading to temporary insanity.

Argumentation

Argumentation

Argumentation is probably the most powerful and most useful of the rhetorical patterns. The objective of an argumentative essay is to persuade the reader to agree with the writer about an issue. There are a few different versions of writing an argumentative essay, but the most common one is discussed on the next page.

Paragraph #1   The introduction

    Attention-getter
    Briefly define and explain the issue.
    State both sides of the issue. (Answer the questions: What is the topic? What is the issue
        or difference of opinion?)
    Thesis statement – State which side of the issue you are on.

Paragraph #2

    Present and discuss one reason why your thesis statement is true.

Paragraph #3

    Present and discuss another reason why your thesis statement is true.

Paragraph #4

    Present and discuss another reason why your thesis statement is true.

Paragraph #5   The opposition

    In this paragraph, explain reasons for the other side of the argument. What would people
    on the other side of the argument say to argue against you?

Paragraph #6   The refutation

    Come back to your side of the argument and explain why the information in paragraph #5
    is wrong or faulty. Try to make your argument in this paragraph stronger than the
    argument in paragraph #5.

Paragraph #7   The conclusion

    Summarize what you have said in paragraphs #2, 3, and 4.

    Restate your thesis statement trying to use different words if possible.

    You MAY provide a solution.

*   *   *   *   *   *   *   *   *   *   *   *   *   *

When a reader is finished reading your essay, the reader should agree with what you said in your thesis statement.

Paragraph #1   The introduction

Attention-getter
Briefly define and explain the issue.
State both sides of the issue. (Answer the questions: What is the topic? What is the
      issue or difference of opinion?)
Thesis statement – State which side of the issue you are on.

Paragraph #2

State and discuss three reasons why your side of the argument is correct.
(Three reasons why your thesis statement is true)

Paragraph #3   opposition

State and discuss reasons why the other side of the issue is right.
What would people argue against you about?

Paragraph #4   refutation

Come back to your side of the argument, and explain why the information in paragraph
#3 is wrong. Try to make your argument in this paragraph stronger than the argument in
paragraph #3. What would you say to counter the ideas of the opposition?

Paragraph #5   conclusion

Summarize what you have said in paragraph #2.

Restate your thesis statement trying to use different words if possible.

You MAY provide a solution.

Paragraph #1   The introduction

     Attention-getter
     Briefly define and explain the issue.
     State both sides of the issue. (Answer the questions: What is the topic? What is the
          issue or difference of opinion?)
     Thesis statement – State which side of the issue you are on.

Paragraph #2

     Present and discuss one reason why your thesis statement is true.

Paragraph #3

     Present and discuss another reason why your thesis statement is true.

Paragraph #4

     Present and discuss anther reason why your thesis statement is true.

Paragraph #5   The conclusion

     Summarize what you have said in paragraphs #2, 3, and 4.

     Restate your thesis statement trying to use different words if possible.

     You MAY provide a solution.

Paragraph #1   The introduction

Attention-getter

Briefly define and explain the issue. State both sides of the issue.

Thesis statement: State which side of the issue you are on.

Paragraph #2

Present a statement about what the opposition (the other side) says about the topic.

Then go to your side and explain why the statement from the other side is wrong.

Paragraph #3

Present another statement about what the opposition (the other side) says about the topic.

Then go to your side and explain why the statement from the other side is wrong.

Paragraph #4

Present another statement about what the opposition (the other side) says about the topic.

Then go to your side and explain why the statement from the other side is wrong.

Paragraph #5   The conclusion

Summarize the ideas about your side of the argument.

Restate your thesis statement trying to use different words if possible.

You MAY provide a solution.

A written dialog can be created in which every assertion can be opposed. However, the goal is the same – to, in the end, win the argument. As for paragraphing, the first paragraph would be the same as the first paragraphs in the other argumentative versions. Then each middle paragraph would contain the writer's assertion and its opposing view. Thus, the argument goes back and forth. Then the last paragraph would be the conclusion, written the same way that the concluding paragraphs are written for the other argumentative versions.

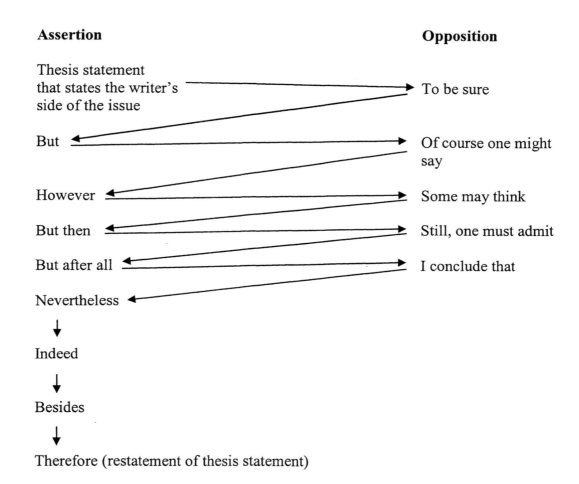

Outline
(Argumentation)

Publish Your Own Book

Thesis statement: Control over art, price, and profit make self-publishing more gratifying and profitable for an author than an author having his or her book published by a conventional publisher.

I. Artistic control
   - A. Author's own ideas   *(my side of argument)
   - B. Author's own way
   - C. Author's own time

II. Price control
   - A. Lower price than conventional publisher   *(my side of argument)
   - B. Higher price than conventional publisher

III. Profit
   - A. Higher percentage of profits for author   *(my side of argument)
   - B. Author markets own book

IV. Conventional publishing
   - A. Credibility   *(opposition – other
   - B. Finances   side of argument)
   - C. Publisher's contacts and experience

V. Self-publishing
   - A. Can build credibility   *(refutation – my side
   - B. Financial options   of argument)
   - C. Can network

VI. Advantages of self-publishing
   - A. Artistic control   *(conclusion)
   - B. Price control
   - C. Profit

*NOTE – When you outline, do not write the words that are in the parentheses ( ).

Publish Your Own Book

There are many ways for a person to earn money. A person might have a skill in writing and a desire to share some of his or her ideas with other people and make money from his or her efforts. If a person writes a book, he or she might consider trying to get a conventional, established publisher like Doubleday to publish the author's manuscript or may decide to self-publish his or her book. A conventional publisher evaluates, edits, prints into book form, and markets an author's manuscript. However, a self-publisher is a person who writes a book, finances it, has it printed, and markets it to the public. Control over art, price, and profit make self-publishing more gratifying and profitable for an author than an author having his or her book published by a conventional publisher.

When an author writes a book and plans to self-publish the book, the author has complete control over what he or she wants to say, the way he or she wants to explain the information, and when he or she wants to say it. For example, a person could write a book about abortion which is a controversial issue. The author could write on the premise that abortion is murder. Such a position might be offensive to pro-choice people. Thus, some conventional publishers might not want to publish such a book because it might offend a large number of possible customers. If an author self-publishes, the writer can write anything he or she wants to. Furthermore, self-publishing allows the writer to phrase his or her words the way he or she wants to because the author is also the editor, so that author will not have to change any of his or her words or ideas because another editor tells him or her to. Also, the author of a self-published book can market the book to the public anytime he or she wants to. For instance, if an author writes a book about how to make various Christmas decorations, the author may want to have the book in book stores in October with the hope of selling more books by longer exposure. A conventional publisher may want to begin marketing the book in mid-November, thinking that longer exposure of the book might cause potential customers to tire of the book before Christmas. If an author self-publishes his or her book, the author can market his or her book whenever he or she wants to.

Another advantage of self-publishing is price control. A self-publisher can establish his or her price for the book lower than a conventional publisher. For example, if a book would sell for $20.00 from a conventional publisher, the self-publisher's comparable book might sell for $16.00 with the hope of selling more books. However, the goal of the self-publisher may be to sell his or her book at a higher price than a conventional publisher. Instead of selling his or her book at $20.00, the author/self-publisher might raise the book's price to $41.00 and include a free gift such as an attractive bookmark. A well written advertisement and/or a beautiful brochure will cause people to buy the book. The author thinks that he or she will sell fewer books but will make a larger profit on each book.

Also, a writer who self-publishes his or her book can make a larger profit than having a conventional publisher publish the book. A self-publisher who works from his or her home has little overhead. An office or room in one's house means that the writer still has to pay rent or a mortgage on the house and utility bills but does not have to pay a separate rent for an office in an office building. By operating from his or her own house or apartment, the author can make a larger profit on his or her book because the author/self-publisher has fewer bills to pay. In addition, an author/self-publisher can make a larger profit by marketing his or her own book. For example, the self-publisher may wish to sell the book through direct mail. The author would then place advertisements in magazines and newspapers that the writer's target audience would tend to read. If an author delivers public speeches, he or she might advertise the book by announcing its existence and have copies of the book available for sale at the sites.

In contrast, conventional publishers can give a writer credibility, finances, and benefits from contacts and experience. Some well established, conventional publishers such as Doubleday have earned prestigious reputations over many years. For an author to get his or her book accepted by a major publisher is an honorable achievement. People who know the author are more likely to be impressed with the author's manuscript if a conventional book publisher thinks that the author's written material is good enough to make a book out of it. In addition to the credibility factor, a conventional publisher also finances the author's book project. The publisher pays for the typesetters, designers, printers and binders. The author has no burden of spending his or her own money or taking a loan which needs to be repaid for getting the actual copies of the book produced. Also, the conventional publisher has all ready established important contacts and much experience in the production of books. Some of the contacts include professionals who provide legal advice, design service, and printing. Conventional publishers also distribute copies of the book to many book stores. Thus, when an author has his or her book produced by a conventional publisher, the author is basically finished with the book project after the author has written the manuscript.

Although conventional publishers can provide the author with various professional services, a self-publisher can accomplish basically the same goals as conventional publishers. With extra effort, the author/self-publisher can gain credibility by including in the book a few paragraphs about the author. The author's credentials such as a college degree and other involvement in activities related to the subject of the book can be stated. If the author does a good job presenting the material in the book, the book will "speak" for itself. People will want to purchase copies of the book to read the information. Presenting workshops on self-publishing to people in various communities will spread the author's expertise in writing and self-publishing. Even though it is true that a self-publisher must provide the cost of getting the book printed and marketed, an author has various financial options. A self-publisher can save money and order possibly a few hundred copies of the book which he or she can distribute to book reviewers and libraries to help the general public become aware of the book. Then when purchase orders come in, the author can use the customers' money to pay to have more books printed. Other initial ways of financing the printing of the book are to borrow the money from a friend or a bank which the author will have to repay plus interest. For marketing the book, the author can network. The author/self-publisher can advertise the book in newspapers and magazines and sell copies of the book through direct mail. He or she can send brochures or free copies of the book for review to book stores to get store owners to stock the books. The author can also contact book clubs. Furthermore, now that computers have become so much of a part of many people's lives, a self-publisher can advertise his or her book over the Internet and reach millions of people. Thus, a self-publisher can build credibility, choose from financial options, and network to sell copies of his or her book.

The author/self-publisher has the freedom to write what he or she wants to write, and how and when he or she wants to write it. The self-publisher also has the choice of selecting a lower or higher price than book stores' selling prices. Finally, by the author selling the book, he or she can earn more profits. Consequently, instead of an author attempting to get a conventional publisher to publish his or her book, the author can self-publish the book, thus having more artistic and price control and reap larger profits, Therefore, self-publishing is more satisfying and lucrative than for an author to have a conventional publisher publish his or her book.

Narration

Narration

A **narrative** essay is **telling a story** about someone or something. The events that took place in the story should usually be written in chronological order, the order in which the events happened in the story. The story will develop the idea in the thesis statement. The story will support and show that the thesis statement idea is true. Begin a new paragraph when you begin a new event in the story (what happened first, what happened second, third, … and what happened last.) Since it is sometimes difficult to find topic sentences for each paragraph in the story, you can start new paragraphs where it seems natural or logical. In the narrative essay in this book, information was put into groups or categorized to start new paragraphs.

Outline

(Narration)

It Happened One Night

Thesis statement: The sinking of the Titanic was a terrible disaster.

I. Setting
   A. Sunday, April 14, 1912
   B. No moon
   C. Sea calm
   D. Stars in sky
   E. Cold
   F. Water 28 degrees F

II. Titanic's collision with iceberg
   A. April 14, 1912, Sunday
   B. 11:40 p.m.
   C. Happened in 10 seconds
   D. 300-Foot gash below waterline
   E. Ship stopped 4 minutes later almost ½ mile
   F. Alarms sounded
   G. Doors between watertight compartments closed
   H. Within 10 minutes water had flooded first 3 holds to 14 feet
   I. Pumps could not take water out fast enough
   J. Lights on until almost end
   K. Watertight compartments
      1. Water fill up
      2. Flow into next compartment
      3. Domino effect
   L. Ship sinking from bow (front)

III. Crew's and passengers' reactions
   A. Captain Smith told John Phillips and Harold Bride, wireless operators, sent distress calls and ship's position
   B. Wireless operators
      1. Californian (British ship)
         a. No contact
         b. 20 miles away
         c. Captain had gone to bed

2. Olympic
    a. Contacted
    b. 500 miles away
3. Carpathia
    a. Contacted
    b. 58 miles away or 5 hours away
    c. Captain Arthur Rostron

C. People assembled on deck – not scared
D. 12:30 a.m. Captain Smith ordered all first and second class passengers to gather on deck.
E. Women and children helped into lifeboats
F. Little panic
G. About 2,200 people on board
H. Lifeboats for 1,178 people
I. Passengers shivering on deck
J. Between 12:45 and 1:45, 8 white rockets lighted and sent up
K. Men said goodbyes to families
L. Some women stayed with husbands
M. Third class steerage passengers forcibly held back in their quarters until most of lifeboats launched

IV. After nearly all regular lifeboats launched, remaining people on board ship
A. Ship noticeably sinking from front
B. Engineers left their posts
C. Stern of ship passengers cling to fixed objects (otherwise washed into icy water)
D. 8 musicians, ships orchestra, kept playing music
E. Lights continued burning until just minutes before entire ship went below water
F. Ship was calm
G. Sea was calm
H. Stern rose further and further out of the water
    1. 2:20 a.m.
    2. Monday, April 15, 1912
    3. 3 propellers swung out of water
    4. Angle of stern increased to 50 degrees
    5. Then 60 degrees
I. Ship began its final plunge
J. Hundreds of people jumped from stern
K. Just before ship went under, large roar
L. Some said ship broke into two
M. Smokestack nearest front fell loose when Titanic sank

V. Rescue
   A. All children first and second class saved except 1
   B. ⅔ steerage went down with ship
   C. Almost all women in first class survived
   D. Nearly ½ of third class women did not survive
   E. 18 lifeboats launched
       1. Stayed clear
       2. 1 went back for survivors
   F. Carpathia ship reached at 4:00 a.m.
   G. Floating wreckage, Titanic gone
   H. 705 survivors got onto Carpathia
   I. Carpathia searched for 4 hours
   J. Captain Rostron positioned ship over where Titanic was assumed to
      have gone down. He called Rev. Anderson, who with rescued passengers,
      paused for service for those who were killed.

It Happened One Night

It was colossal! It was the largest and most luxurious ship in the world. Many people thought it was unsinkable. This ship was powerful and exquisite. This ship was the Titanic. It boasted four smokestacks, three to carry off smoke and steam and one to ventilate. Each smokestack was 62 feet high and wide enough for 2 train locomotives to fit side by side into each. The Titanic weighed 46,328 gross tons and had a length equivalent to 4 city blocks. It was almost as high as an eleven-story building. This vessel carried 3,500 bags of mail and 900 tons of baggage. The Titanic was built in 1912 at a cost of $10 million. The gorgeous staterooms and the spacious public rooms and parlors had deep carpets, pianos, easy chairs, and great sofas. This great ship contained a cafeteria, swimming pools, gymnasium, and squash court which were just some of the ship's features. There was even a daily newspaper published every morning. With the ship filled to 60% of its capacity, there were approximately 2,224 people on the Titanic – at least 1,316 passengers and 892 crew members. There were 3 classes of passengers. The first-class members included such people as Colonel John Jacob Astor, the richest man on the ship, and his pregnant wife; Mr. and Mrs. Isador Straus, the owners of Macy's Department Store; and President Taft's military aide, Major Archibald Butt. There was also a second class of passengers. The third-class passengers, or steerage passengers, were assigned to the bottom of the ship. The Titanic's first and only voyage began in Southampton, England, on April 10, 1912, and after crossing the Atlantic Ocean was to arrive in New York. The sinking of the Titanic was a terrible disaster.

Even though the ship's officers had received a few warnings of icebergs in the area, the night seemed rather peaceful. It was Sunday, April 14, 1912, the fourth day of the trip. No moon shown in the sky, but many stars were bright. It was cold. The ocean was calm but 28 degrees Fahrenheit which was below freezing.

The disaster struck at 11:40 p.m. that night of April 14th. One of the two lookouts in the crow's nest saw a huge iceberg ahead. He immediately rang the ship's warning bells 3 times and telephoned the bridge that an iceberg was straight ahead. The sixth officer relayed the message to First Officer Murdoch who was in charge after Captain E. J. Smith had retired for the night. Murdoch immediately ordered all of the engines stopped and then put into reverse. Then he told the quartermaster to turn the wheel to the left. As he was giving these orders, he flipped the switch to shut the watertight doors. Alarms sounded. The big ship continued straight ahead for about 30 seconds and then turned slightly to the left. The warning from the crow's nest was too late to completely miss the iceberg. As the Titanic cruised by the iceberg, the ship scraped its right side for about 10 seconds against the iceberg, either tearing a 300-foot gash or buckling and tearing off some of the metal sheathing below the waterline. Murdoch felt a little bump and then a grinding noise below. When Captain Smith heard the grinding noise too, he immediately went from his room to the bridge. Murdoch informed Captain Smith of the situation. The captain ordered the ship to be stopped. The ship took 4 minutes to completely stop traveling and almost ½ mile from where the collision had occurred. Within 10 minutes, ocean water had flooded the first 3 compartments to 14 feet. The pumps could not take out the water fast enough. As the watertight compartments filled to capacity, the water flowed into the next compartment, creating a "domino effect," like if one end of an ice cube tray was submerged in water. The ship began sinking from the front. The lights remained on.

At first, some of the crew members realized the danger of the damage, but the passengers were unaware or calm just after the collision. Captain Smith told the two wireless operators, John Phillips and Harold Bride, to send distress calls and the ship's position to officers of other ships. Phillips and Bride contacted 2 ships: the Olympic which was 500 miles away, and the Carpathia which was 58 miles or 5 hours away. The Carpathia's captain, Arthur Rostron, ordered his crew to press the ship full steam ahead, racing toward the Titanic. As contact was being made with other ships, some of the passengers of the Titanic assembled on the deck but did not seem scared. At 12:30 a.m., Captain Smith ordered all first and second-class passengers to gather onto the deck. With life jackets on, as women and children were helped into lifeboats, there was still little panic. The problem was that there were about 2,200 people on the Titanic, but there were lifeboats enough for only 1,178 people. The cold air made the passengers shiver on deck. Between 12:45 a.m. and 1:45 a.m., crew members of the Titanic shot up 8 white rockets as distress signals to light the sky. The closest ship, the British ship, the Californian, was only 20 miles away, but the captain had gone to bed, and the ship's wireless had been shut down for the night. It is not known if the Californian's crew was close enough to have seen the rockets which were universal distress signals. Meanwhile, on the Titanic, as some women and children were getting into the lifeboats, men said goodbyes to their families. Some women would not leave their husbands behind such as Mrs. Isador Straus. She said, "I've always stayed with my husband. Why should I leave him now? We've been living together for many years. Where you go, I go." Third-class passengers did not have options at that time. They were being forcibly held back in their quarters until most of the lifeboats had been launched. At 1:55 a.m. there were 1,500 people still on board the Titanic. As the last few regular lifeboats were being lowered into the water, the only remaining boats were 2 to 4 canvas, collapsible lifeboats that could each hold 47 people.

At this point in time, for the people left on the ship, it was mostly every person for himself or herself. Captain Smith told the two wireless operators, Phillips and Bride, that they were free to leave their posts. Stewards unlocked the gates for the steerage passengers who quickly ran to the upper decks. Engineers left their posts, and some first-class and second-class members were still on board. The crowd turned into an unruly mob. As regular lifeboat number 14 was being loaded with people, a group of other passengers ran to the boat, but the crew held them off with the ship's tiller. When another group began advancing to the boat, Fifth Officer Lowe pulled out a pistol. While firing his pistol 3 times into the air, he shouted, "If anyone else tries that, this is what he'll get!" As some of the crew members held off the crowd, some other crew members continued lowering the regular lifeboats. The Titanic continued sinking from the front so that the deck of the ship kept tilting more and more. Normally the boat deck was 70 feet above the water. At this time, the boat deck was only about 15 feet from the water. The remaining passengers on the Titanic scrambled to the back of the ship and clung onto any objects that were fixed such as the ship's railing to keep from sliding down the tilting deck into the icy water. Eight musicians kept playing music throughout this ordeal to try to keep the passengers calm. They stopped playing just before the Titanic completely went under water. The ship's lights remained on until just a few minutes before the entire ship went below the water. The ship became more and more vertical, and the sea remained calm. The stern, or back of the ship, rose further and further out of the water. At 2:20 a.m., Monday, April 15, 1912, the 3 propellers swung out of the water. The angle of the ship's stern increased to 50 degrees, then 60 degrees. The Titanic began its final plunge. Hundreds of people jumped from the ship into the icy water, and hundreds of more people were stuck inside of the ship. The band stopped playing. The lights flickered once, came back on, and then went off permanently. The stern was almost vertical and inside dishware, furniture, cargo, and machinery plunged toward the front of the ship. Survivor Lawrence Beesley described the awful and loud noise: "It was partly a roar, partly a groan, partly a rattle, partly a smash, and it was not a sudden roar as an explosion would be; it went on successively for some seconds, possibly fifteen to twenty, as heavy machinery dropped down to the ... bow of the ship.... But it was a noise no one had heard before, and no one wishes to hear again; it was stupefying, stupendous, as it came to us along the water." Finally, the terrific noise ended. The stern of the ship slid down at a slant, picking up speed as it went, until the Titanic disappeared completely beneath the water. Some people said as the Titanic was going down that the ship broke in two and that the smokestack nearest the front fell loose. All that was left was wreckage. People tried to hold onto deck chairs and any other debris that would help them to stay afloat.

The rescue efforts saved some people's lives but not others. People in the 18 lifeboats that had been launched had rowed far away from the ship, afraid that as the Titanic completely sank, it might create a suction that would take some of the lifeboats with it. People in lifeboats could hear cries for help from those people in the water. Titanic's Fifth Officer Lowe managed to locate 4 partially filled boats. He tied these boats together and put his passengers into the other boats and took his boat back to where the Titanic had been to try to save some survivors. When he heard occasional cries in the darkness, by the time he reached these people, it was usually too late to save them because people could not survive long in the freezing water. At 4:00 a.m., the ship, the Carpathia, reached the floating wreckage where the Titanic had sunk. Seven hundred, five survivors got onto the Carpathia. Among the survivors were wireless operator, Harold Bride and millionairess Molly Brown who had taken over one of the lifeboats and became known as "The Unsinkable Molly Brown." The Carpathia searched for more survivors for 4 hours. Then the Carpathia's captain, Arthur Rostron, positioned the Carpathia over where the Titanic was assumed to have gone down. He then called Rev. Anderson to conduct a service for the people who had not survived and for those people who had. Among the people who did not survive were wireless operator, John Phillips, and the designer of the Titanic, Thomas Andrews. There are a few stories as to what had happened to Captain E. J. Smith of the Titanic during the disaster, but it is assumed that he perished. A few days later the ship, Mackay-Bennett, spent 2 weeks searching the water in the area of the wreckage. The crew found more than 300 dead bodies. Among them was the frozen body of John Jacob Astor. Totally, more than 1,500 people had last their lives from the sinking of the Titanic.

In 1912 the Titanic was the largest and most comfortable, ornate ship of its time. While traveling on its maiden voyage through the icy waters of the North Atlantic from Southampton, England, to New York, on Sunday, April 14, 1912, this huge ship struck an iceberg which tore a hole in the right side of the ship below the waterline. As the Titanic began sinking, many people who had gotten into the lifeboats survived, but most of the people on board perished with the Titanic. In the early hours of Monday, April 15, 1912, the Titanic plunged to the ocean floor. About 4:00 a.m., the rescue ship, the Carpathia, arrived. Seven hundred, five Titanic survivors boarded the Carpathia. More than 1,500 other Titanic crew members and passengers were killed. The sinking of the Titanic was a horrible event.

Essay / Research Paper

Similarities & Differences

Similarities

* Same Structure / Same Parts

      * Introduction including thesis statement

      * Middle Paragraphs   (As many as you want)

        Topic Sentence followed by Supportive Evidence (details/examples)

      * Conclusion

        Summary   (Restate ideas in topic sentences
                      from middle paragraphs.)

        Restate thesis statement idea.

Differences

* A research paper is a

      * longer

      * more detailed

      * documented

Essay.